THE
HEALTHY
SOFTWARE
PROJECT

THE
HEALTHY SOFTWARE PROJECT

A GUIDE TO SUCCESSFUL DEVELOPMENT AND MANAGEMENT

Mark Norris, Peter Rigby and **Malcolm Payne**

BT, UK

JOHN WILEY & SONS

Chichester • New York • Brisbane • Toronto • Singapore

Other Wiley Editorial Offices

John Wiley & Sons, Inc., 605 Third Avenue,
New York, NY 10158-0012, USA

Jacaranda Wiley Ltd, G.P.O. Box 859, Brisbane,
Queensland 4001, Australia

John Wiley & Sons (Canada) Ltd, 22 Worcester Road,
Rexdale, Ontario M9W 1L1, Canada

John Wiley & Sons (SEA) Pte Ltd, 37 Jalan Pemimpin #05-04,
Block B, Union Industrial Building, Singapore 2057

Library of Congress Cataloging-in-Publication Data

Norris, Mark.
   The healthy software project : a guide to successful development and
management / Mark Norris, Peter Rigby, Malcolm Payne.
      p.   cm.
   Includes bibliographical references (p.   ) and index.
   ISBN 0 471 94042-9
   1. Computer software—Development.   I. Rigby, Peter.   II. Payne, Malcolm.
   III. Title.
QA76.76.D47N65   1993
005.1—dc20   93–10573
   for DLC   CIP

British Library Cataloguing in Publication Data

A catalogue record for this book is available from the British Library

ISBN 0 471 94042 9

Typeset in 10/12pt Palatino from author's disks by Text Processing Department,
John Wiley & Sons Ltd, Chichester
Printed and bound in Great Britain by Bookcraft (Bath) Ltd

Contents

Preface

This book aims to present an ordered collection of learning points from past software projects. The basic idea is that the same mistakes tend to be made over and over again. Also, these mistakes are solved in much the same way by successive generations of project managers, team leaders and customers, who learn by painful experience. Our purpose in writing this text is to minimise that pain by helping to avoid some of the classic mistakes and, even if things have gone awry, to advise on how best to restore the situation.

The medical analogy developed through the book evolved as it became clear to the authors that the concepts of sickness, recovery and health apply as readily to software projects as they do to people. There are reproducible symptoms that precede sickness and there are known medicines that will cure specific ailments. Just as a good medical practitioner can quickly diagnose a patient and prescribe a course of treatment, so this book should help in spotting a sick project and in getting it back on its feet.

The intended readership is therefore fairly broad. The practical bias of the information here would be of use in the first instance to the managers and customers of software projects. Given that projects only really succeed if all the people involved are properly focussed and committed, we would like to think that everyone who has embarked on a career in software (or is about to do so) will dip into this text. Hopefully for information—if nothing else, for a good read.

Foreword

Software lies at the core of many modern systems. The ability to manage the development of complex software systems is one of the most daunting challenges facing engineers in this decade and probably well into the future.

Tens of millions of pounds have been invested in the development of software technology to facilitate the development process. The concepts of engineering lifecycles and quality management have been deployed with the aim of improving the chances of successful development.

Even so, and despite considerable progress, many of the traditional textbook approaches to software development and management do not help. The main reason for this is that they are based on the fallacy that the normal situation facing software engineers is one of a 'green field site'. Rarely are managers or developers faced with such a sitaution, especially in the area of large systems developments. In telecommunications, for instance, functionality depends on integrated sets of systems.

A critical issue facing software managers is, therefore, how to manage developments based on systems that have been in place for some time—in particular, how to revitalise such software developments.

This concept, sometimes called the recovery of software projects, is a key theme of this book. The experience of many managers and engineers is evident in the presentation and analysis of software recovery presented here. Recognition of the need for recovery and the disciplined implementation of a recovery plan are often crucial in ensuring the successful delivery of major software projects. Failure to recognise the symptoms presented in this book often results in unrealistic committment to dates and functionality on the part of managers whose engineers are only too aware that they are impossible to meet. It is this scenario that has led to the failure of many major software projects in recent years.

Finally, software engineering and the management of software projects remain two of the most exacting challenges in modern business. The topics discussed in this book will not only provide guidance on how to meet these challenges but also help readers actually enjoy overcoming the pitfalls of the software project.

Sinclair Stockman
BT

About the Authors

Mark Norris has over 15 years' experience of a broad range of software and communications ventures. On the way he has managed several dozen projects to completion, from the very small to the multi-million pound, multi-site. He runs a unit that has operated to the ISO9001 standard for the last four years and was one of the first software units in Europe to be registered. Mark has published extensively over the last ten years, has worked for periods in Japan and Australia and is a member of the IEE professional group on software engineering. In line with his belief in learning from the experiences of others, he has initiated several courses within BT based on software project case studies.

Peter Rigby has for many years been involved in quality management systems. He has been the quality manager for at least two software organisations within BT when they were accredited to the ISO9001 standard and is actively involved in software quality projects and forums. Most of Peter's work focuses on capability assessment of software suppliers. He is currently engaged in the production of BT's software capability and assessment method.

Malcolm Payne has worked in a procurement function for over 20 years and has extensive experience of software development and implementation projects. For the last 4 years he has been instrumental in developing methods for improving the acquisition processes used by BT for software-rich systems. Malcolm's main interests lie in the areas of process assessment, contractural frameworks and customer/supplier models. His work involves him in many multi-million pound software projects from an international supply base.

Acknowledgements

The authors would like to thank several people whose cooperation and forebearance have helped with this book.

To those brave souls who reviewed the early drafts of the book—Sinclair Stockman, Trevor Matthews, Darius Karkaria, Dave Sutherland, Catriona Mackie, John Foster, Ray Lewis, Alan Stoddart, Mike Tilley and Alan Redhead. Their constructive criticism has been welcome, valuable and (on occasions) downright amusing. To Dr Richard Stocks Consultant Paediatrician for his advice and guidance on the medical analogy.

To our many friends and colleagues in BT's Software Development, Technology and Procurement units whose experience, advice and inside stories have been invaluable (and, in some cases, too interesting to publish!).

Last, but not least, our wives, Fiona, Liz and Viv, for their forebearance, patience and support throughout. A special mention also to Kate, Amy and Adam (from MN) for not deleting some of the master files before they were backed up!

1

The Healthy Software Project

The customer may not always be right
but the customer is always … the customer

CW Moore

Software projects are far from perfect. They certainly deliver what the customer wanted more often than they used to but, given that they are increasingly critical to the safety and prosperity of the people who develop and use them, improvements are still necessary. This book seeks to contribute to that improvement.

The authors have been involved with many software rich projects over the years, most of which delivered some form of end product. In retrospect some of these projects were widely regarded as successful, others were deemed failures. But it wasn't simply whether they delivered or not that discriminated the good projects from the rest. There is a qualitative difference between good and bad projects that is not difficult to spot once you have seen enough of them to completion.

The luxury of hindsight is not open to most people, though. Ideally, one would like to be able to recognise at an early stage the signs of a healthy project and, perhaps more importantly, their absence. This book explores the healthy software project or, more specifically, how to recognise and recover a sick one.

For reasons that will become apparent as this text unfolds, a healthy or successful project is defined as one that:

● meets the customers perceived requirements;

● makes the customer want to come back with more business;

● allows the product to be delivered leaving the supplier fit and able to continue future production.

There are many things that contribute to success but, in essence, these can be covered by three key factors—the way in which the project is run, the quality of the product itself and, most important of all, the contribution of all of the people involved in the project.

First, a few relevant definitions—what do we mean by a 'project' and who are the 'customer' and 'supplier'?

1.1   PROJECTS, SUPPLIERS AND CUSTOMERS

Classically, software development is described in the form of a project—an ordered sequence of tasks and interim products—that is an entity in its own right. This notion of a project is common to many other activities as it provides a convenient and manageable way of achieving a particular aim or objective [Loc88].

The idea of the project is very simple. It exists because someone wants the end product and (normally) the associated deliverables that are built in evolving the product (e.g. a software package plus the associated documentation, the developer's kit, the helpdesk, etc).

In essence this means that there must exist a customer for the project, and hence the project team can be seen as the supplier of the product and its associated deliverables. Many excellent books have already been written on project management, and the mechanics of how to plan, control and monitor a project are well understood and widely practised. Even so, supplier–project–customer interaction is, in reality, very complex: a point illustrated later in this text. For a project to be healthy it is not enough to ensure procedural correctness. A logical approach to understanding and resolving these interactions needs to be taken and the customers aspirations need to be actively managed [Boe89].

The interaction between the customer and supplier is examined later. For now it is important to realise that a project—any project—does not exist in isolation and must have some level of customer interaction if it is to succeed. The point is that it is the *right* level and style of interaction that needs to be established [Elp92].

At one end of the spectrum is minimal interaction. In this case requirements are defined and criteria for end product acceptance are agreed. More usually the level of interaction is more complex and there is extensive interaction with the customer. This has direct impact on the health of the project and a balance needs to be struck, as illustrated in Figure 1.1. This diagram gives a simple picture of the factors that need to be held in balance for a project to succeed. Too much pull in either direction will ultimately jeopardise the long term health of the project.

Once an operational balance is achieved, the next challenge for any project is to meet the perceived customer requirements. To do this, a number of demands have to be met, some explicit in the form of defined functional and

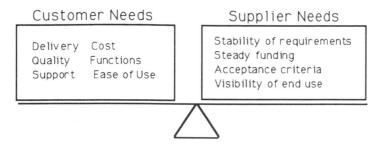

Figure 1.1   A model of customer/supplier relationships

qualitative specifications, others implied but nonetheless vital to the successful conclusion of the project. This set of 'unspoken' requirements needs to be realised if total customer satisfaction is to be achieved [Gil87].

With increasing competition, the need to generate repeat business is ever more important [Mon89]. And that will only be achieved through projects that achieve operational balance *and* meet both explicit and implicit customer needs.

The definition of projects given here gives rise to a number of viewpoints on how the challenge can be met. Several commonly held views of how to manage projects involve balancing three key parameters—two favourites are illustrated in Figure 1.2. The first, (a) is often used as part of software management courses, the other (b) is the basis of action-centred leadership [Ada86]. Both are useful but neither covers all the bases that are actually needed for most software projects.

The theme developed through the course of this book is similar to both of the above ideas but is driven primarily by observation of real projects. Again, there are three parameters that need to be continually attended to. For software projects, our experience is that the most relevant three are the

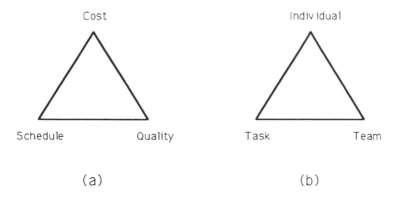

Figure 1.2   Two views of the balance of concerns within a project

people who are involved in the project, the process or procedures that they follow and the product itself. We now proceed to explain this further.

1.2   THE PEOPLE, THE PROCESS AND THE PRODUCT

These three key factors apply for any type of project. They are particularly important to consider in software projects because firm standards in all three areas have yet to be established. The control and balance of the People, the Process and the Product in software projects is crucial to success.

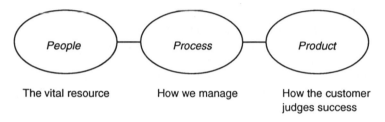

Figure 1.3   The three keys to a successful project

If you keep the three Ps described here under control and manage the way in which they interact, you will have a healthy and, in time, a successful project. But this is not a mechanistic affair. A healthy project can quickly become ill and prolonged illness can lead to failure. The important point is that the symptoms of ill health need to be recognised and remedied as soon as possible.

One of the main objectives of this book is to explain why software projects (in particular) often go wrong, what the symptoms and root causes are, and what can be done to bring them back on track. The first step towards this, in the next chapter, will be to consider what it is about software projects that makes them different.

1.3   THE PLAYERS

So far we have run through the key drivers for healthy software projects. Before moving on into the detail of what can and should be done in each area, we need to determine who needs to do it. In other words, who are the players?

Earlier on we introduced the role of the customer—the person who pays for and (perhaps) uses the product delivered by the software project. Since every customer must have a supplier, there are at least two key players that need to be considered. Unfortunately, life is rarely that simple and the roles of customer/user and supplier/developer are not usually that clear cut.

Rather than trying to define the roles of supplier, user, customer, etc, we need to look at the way in which a software project operates as this has a significant effect on who needs to do what.

From the authors' experience, there appear to be five general levels of acquisition that help determine the appropriate balance of the three Ps. These are:

- The single team. In this case the supplier consists of a team of people who all work in the same organisational unit. The team leader is usually the project manager. Perhaps the most important issue in this instance is to develop the capability of the team since this is the currency for continued success. People issues dominate in a single team.

- The matrix team. This is similar to the single team bar the fact that there is less need to build team capability as composition will change from project to project. The control over (possibly) different ways of operation is important in a matrix team. People issues are still important but process is also key.

- The contract team. In this case, responsibility for the project to deliver rests more with the team leader/project manager. This can be difficult to control directly, especially if reliance for innovative input is placed on a team assembled on a hire and fire basis. The process and product issues begin to dominate here.

- Outsourced supply. This is an extreme example of the contract team—not only is the team bought in but they are also physically remote from the project manager. Process control is vital here

- Procured supply. The ultimate in outsourcing is the purchase of completed software packages. By this stage all but product and support issues have passed.

From the customer viewpoint, there is always some choice over how the project is set up. Even so, it is still important to know what the key issues are for each. Procuring a product might seem easy but it is not always that straightforward to get exactly what you want—and the supplier might not fix the product for the customer if it goes wrong at a later date.

The use of local single teams has significant benefits, particularly for the management of ill-defined requirements and especially for strategically important systems. Typically, this is most appropriate when considering possible competitive advantage. However, a considerable amount of effort is needed in these situations to ensure that the right product is developed.

1.4   SICKNESS AND HEALTH

The analogy between software projects and medical practice will be developed throughout the course of this book. The next chapter starts this off by looking at the special characteristics and problems of software projects. Some software projects—good, bad and average—are reviewed in Chapter 3 to illustrate some of the more common aspects of what really happens.

Chapter 4 looks at some of the early warning signs that a project is sick—the symptoms of ill health. Chapter 5 outlines the tools and techniques (medicine) that is available for treatment. Chapter 6 brings these two together by advising on the appropriate treatment for a given set of symptoms. Finally, we outline a case of a sick project that was recovered and give a programme for continued good health. The detection of sickness and routes to good health are described throughout in terms of people, process and product.

The book is a guide to success in software projects—the key points to look for and what to do if you see them. It is not just for those who manage projects but also for the customer who wants to get a firm grip on progress and for the team members who, like good first-aiders, are closest to the action and often best equipped to see what needs to be done. As this text unfolds we aim to show that there are others who are more than software project first-aiders. There are also general practitioners, surgeons, midwives, even coroners.

1.5   SUMMARY

If you are responsible for producing software, then how well are you doing? Could you be more competitive? Could some problems be prevented before they happen? Even if you are contracting someone else to produce a software-rich system for you, you need to be sure that they provide exactly what you want. And it is no easy task to monitor the function, the quality and the cost of a complex product. Software projects are notoriously difficult to control—success is possible but elusive.

The two basic ideas introduced in this chapter that begin to help explain how to achieve this were:

- A healthy or successful project is defined as one that meets the customers' perceived requirements, makes them want to come back with more business and allows the product to be delivered leaving the supplier fit and able to continue with future production.

- The control and balance of the People, the Process and the Product in software projects is crucial to success. A model that contains these three critical ingredients for successful software projects is explained.

Using these simple ideas and a little hindsight, we can begin to explore the key parameters that need to be managed in order to keep software projects on track.

This is no simple matter though and there is no way to *ensure* a healthy project. But there are signs and symptoms that you should be aware of, common ailments that should be guarded against and common remedies that can be used to good effect.

Later chapters elaborate on this basic pattern by describing some real projects, and analysing what was good and bad about the way they were handled. From this, some more general pointers to the early warning signs of an ailing project are given. By analogy with medical practice, the available techniques for dealing with a set of known symptoms are discussed and guidelines to their application given.

The main point of this chapter is that it is possible for software projects to become sick. Once this happens they have to be treated just as a doctor would treat a sick patient. Treatment is complicated by the nature of the product and by the variety of ways in which it is developed but to be successful demands that the project is kept healthy.

REFERENCES

[Ada86] Adair J (1986) *Action Centred Leadership* Gower Press

[Boe89] Boehm B (1989) *Software Risk Management* IEEE Computer Society Press

[Elp92] Elphick B (1992) Linking the use of resources to project process *Engineering Management Journal*, Dec

[Gil87] Gilb T (1987) *Design by Objectives* North-Holland

[Loc88] Lock D (1988) *Project Management* Gower Press

[Mon89] Monk P (1989) *Technological Change in the Information Economy* Pinter

2

What's so Different about Software?

If you open that Pandora's box,
you never know what Trojan horses will jump out

Ernest Bevin

On the face of it, software engineering is merely a new activity to which the traditional skills and standards of engineering need to be applied. To some extent, this is true and many of the observations contained in this book would apply just as well to a bridge-building project. There are some aspects of software development, though, that are different. This chapter starts by highlighting the main differences and the problems that these can cause. Having identified some of the fundamental challenges of software projects, we move on to see how they can be tackled. The three-P framework is developed a little further here to illustrate where we are and what can be done [NR92].

2.1 TRADEMARKS OF THE PRODUCT

The components with which the more established branches of engineering operate are visible, tangible and can be produced to a measurable standard. Mechanical and electrical parts have precise qualities—a 4 mm nut fits a 4 mm bolt, a 50 volt source causes 1 Ampere to flow when connected across a 50 ohm resistor.

The components of software are not so easy to define. They may or may not consist of objects, files, algorithms, modules, forms and screens. These entities themselves consist of words, symbols, formulae or even some other concept derived from natural language.

Hence the first differentiator in software projects, the product, is difficult to visualise. The impact of this is that reproducible measures and standards are difficult to define. For example, something as straightforward as the number of statements in the simple program below, written in the popular C language, is open to considerable interpretation.

```
#define   LOWER 0
#define   UPPER 300
#define   STEP 20

main ()
{
    int fahr;
    for (fahr=LOWER; fahr<=UPPER; fahr=fahr+STEP)
        printf("%4d %6.1f\n", fahr, (5.0/9.0*(fahr-32)));
}
```

When a group of experienced practitioners were asked (at a software measurement meeting) how many statements there were in this simple programme, there was an interesting lack of consensus. Figure 2.1 shows the distribution of answers received. Clearly, measures of software are, like those of beauty, very much in the eye of the beholder.

Given that even simple portions of software are open to such interpretation, it is little wonder that the product is difficult to describe accurately. One of the important consequences of this is that software standards are far from uniform in their interpretation. No matter how precise a definition may appear (and even mathematically formal definitions are open to some

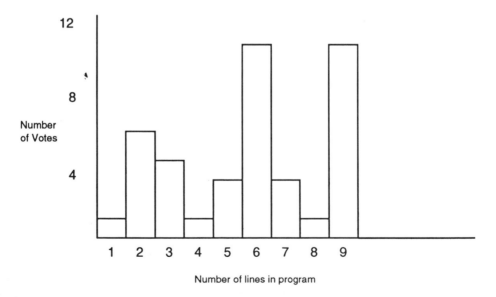

Figure 2.1   A range of opinions on a software measure

degree of interpretation), any guarantees of interoperability or of conformance to specification are difficult to ensure. There is some way to go before we have the equivalent of the software 4 mm nut and bolt!

A second differentiator with software projects is that there is no tangible end product: the software product is all words and pictures. Some product is formal (e.g. code), some descriptive (e.g. designs) but it is all text of some form [Fre87].

People are not adept at producing engineering products based on natural language. They are predisposed to learn and use spoken language but written expression only matures in the environment of an established literature. Witness the evolution of modern text from earlier forms (such as hieroglyphics) that predate ancient civilisations.

Given that software engineering is only just over 30 years old, it is hardly surprising that a rich and mature literature, from which engineers can learn, is yet not in place. The move from art to science may have started for software but it still has some way to go.

In this current state of immaturity, software mistakes are easy to make. Names for modules, arrays, variables and objects are easily confused or forgotten. Complex logic is easy to get wrong—often subtly enough for problems to be found only much later.

The problem is amply illustrated in practice. A recent piece of navigation software, loaded into a space probe, had one line of its code entered as Id =1.10 instead of Id = 1,10, This turned an intended loop into a variable assignment and caused a multi-million pound project to, literally, miss its target.

Even the simplest of assignments can become troublesome when one of the more popular languages in current use allows:

```
for (;P("\n"), R=;P("|"))
for (e=C;e=;P("_"+(*u++/8)%2))P("| "+(*u/4)%2);
```

as a legal statement. The comment that was associated with this statement defied anyone to work out what it did. Fortunately, that module never required modification!

To reiterate, the key points being made here are:

● The detail of software matters. One mistake can make the difference between success and failure and it is difficult to state what is required with both clarity and precision.

● The intangible nature of software make it *inherently* error prone. The customers rarely get exactly what they think they have asked for.

Put these two factors together with the sheer complexity of modern systems and it is no great surprise that traditional engineering project management does not transfer altogether successfully. This is the third problem: it is not at all clear how software *should* be developed. There are many recommended practices but little evidence that they produce the desired end result. A good process does not necessarily lead to a good product (and vice versa).

This is no reason to be too despondent, though. There may be no set algorithm for proper software, but there are many symptoms to watch for and remedies that can be (and have been) applied. Software projects *can* be controlled but good project management practice needs to be supplemented.

The word 'healthy' in the title of this text is not chosen by chance. Many of the experience-based observations contained in later chapters can (and have been) applied to projects just as a doctor would prescribe medicine for a patient. The analogies of sickness, diagnosis, recovery and health all exist in software projects. Subsequent chapters are based very much around this analogy and draw on a range of project experiences to provide a set of tools to help the manager, customer and engineer.

Given that each project has its own complexities, we can do no more than skim here. We will, however, abstract from this to concentrate on the outward signs that indicate inner health and the range and currency of available cures.

2.2   ARE SOFTWARE PROJECTS THAT IMPORTANT?

There is little point in seeking a cure for a minor ailment that will in time go away. So the next question, in the title of this section, has to be addressed before we continue.

The need for healthier software projects can be illustrated by looking at a few trends taken from published strategic reports [ACA86]. Some of the more striking points made are:

- Software currently accounts for about 5% of the UK gross national product and given the trends over the last ten years, this is more likely to rise than abate.

- The proportion of IT costs attributable to software rose from 40% in 1980 to 80% in 1990.

- The European software services market, estimated at 40B Ecu in 1990 is set to rise to more than 60B Ecu by 1993.

In addition to these gross size figures, these strategic reports have identified a number of key problems, the main ones being [Hob90]:

- On average, large software systems are delivered a year behind schedule.

- Only 1% of major software projects finish on time, to budget and deliver what the customer wanted.

- 25% of all software-intensive projects never finish at all.

- Over 60% of IT product managers have little or no experience of modern best software engineering practice.

The effects of the above factors have been estimated, in cost terms, to be of the order of two billion pounds a year in the UK alone.

So, the patient is not that healthy and some restorative action is required!

2.3 PEOPLE, PROCESSES AND PRODUCTS

Armed with the caveat that software projects have their own special challenges, we return to the idea that success is a question of managing the key drivers—the people, the process and the product. A major part of success in software projects lies in balancing these three. Looking again at their interaction, Figure 2.2, the only way to win is if all three are well enough understood and controlled—if any one of the drivers is ignored then the likelihood of a satisfactory end result is significantly diminished.

If all three of the factors shown above were understood, software projects would be controlled and scientific affairs. This is currently not the case but there are some important pointers towards that ideal:

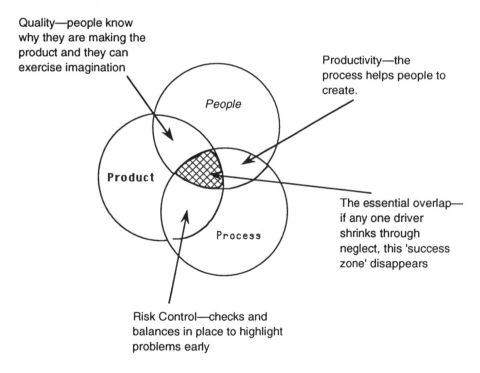

Figure 2.2 The interaction between the three drivers of the healthy project

- The intersection of process and product is the aim of risk-based project management—ensuring that the business process of delivering a relevant product is monitored and that corrections of course are made.

- The area of overlap between the people and the product is all about providing the non-functional requirements, such as usability, reliability and maintainability, that can dominate a customer's perception of quality.

- The overlap between the people and the process is what Quality Management Systems should aim to address. They should provide a framework that guides people in doing their job—not introduce artificial constraints just because 'that's what the QMS says'.

The extent to which each of the three aims is satisfied by current practice and techniques will be one of the threads running through the book.

Perhaps the best understood of the three Ps in the context of software development is the process—all the different stages involved in making a software product, from requirements capture through to design, testing, maintenance and replacement. The mechanics here are now well known and have been extensively documented (in standards such as ISO9001 and in practices such as Total Quality Management).

The software product, like the process, has also been widely studied and there are many different ways in which it can be characterised: measures of size, complexity, information flow, test coverage, etc, can be readily gathered automatically. There are many ways of measuring the product (and this refers not only to the source code but also to the support documentation, test documentation and anything else that is required to keep the code in line with the customer's requirements).

Many product measures, though, are currently offered by the Snake Oil Salesmen of the software industry, the consultants and the tool vendors, with very little evidence that what can be measured is in fact useful to measure.

The last of the three Ps—the people—often receives less attention than either the process or the product. Here we mean *all* of the people involved, directly or indirectly, in the project from customer, through developer, to user. Each can significantly influence success or failure and the behaviour of each needs to be considered under this heading.

Now that we have defined the constituent parts of Figure 2.2, we can start to look at the key issues inside each one.

The software process

In theory, the software process is very ordered and controlled. For many years now, there have been defined 'lifecycles' which purport to describe the various stages of software development. As well as these well defined technical processes, there is a wealth of information on the quality control techniques that are available to manage software projects.

In practice, most software developments bear only a passing resemblance to the published 'lifecycles' and the so-called quality control procedures are sometimes more concerned with damage limitation than guaranteeing quality in the end product.

This is something of a pessimistic assessment but it is not without basis. Although Quality Management Systems (QMS) are now commonplace in software organisations, few people would claim that they ensure a quality product [NR92]. A QMS validated to a recognised standard such as ISO9001/BS5750 provides a basic level of project control, but no more. The fitness for purpose of the end product still relies on the commitment of the people who produce it. And it is not unknown for a QMS to inhibit rather than enable this. Even so, process is generally recognised as a key aspect of quality. The European Quality Award is built very much on process as a key building block (albeit not directly related to the product quality).

Registration to ISO9001 has, for many, become a target in its own right. There has been little examination of the real impact of a QMS on the overall health of a project. There is little question that you need some measure of control (e.g. configuration management procedures) but the processes defined in the QMS as a whole should enable rather than inhibit. They need to be built around what actually needs to be done to produce the product. They also need to ensure that people are allowed to create, which is what software engineering is all about. The problem is that the current standards (or, more accurately, their interpretation) tend towards the bureaucratic.

This more complete view of project effectiveness is what lies behind Total Quality Management (TQM). The focus is on understanding where you are

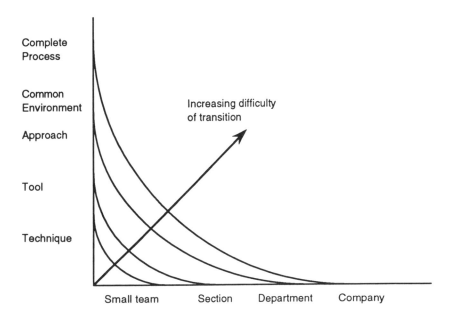

Figure 2.3   The challenge of change

and moving forward—changing and improving how something is done, based on how effective the current method is (or isn't) in practice.

In terms of addressing the real issue of quality, this is a step forward from laying down a fixed set of procedures in a QMS. Its strength lies in the fact that the people who perceive the need for improvement are those who identify how it should be done. Even so, changes are not easy. This is particularly true if those changes are large ones.

The difficulty of implementing change is illustrated in Figure 2.3.

Small local changes are fairly easy to implement. The introduction of a small change across a large company takes time and effort. So too does the reworking of a complete process for a small team. Changing the way a whole company works can be a lifetime achievement.

Tilleys law—that any initiative slows down by a factor of ten for every level that it is elevated within an organisation—should not be underestimated!

Even so, there is significant evidence that the need for change is recognised and that a significant (and growing) number of organisations are taking action. Figure 2.4 shows the number of formal process assessments to the recognised SEI format over the last few years.

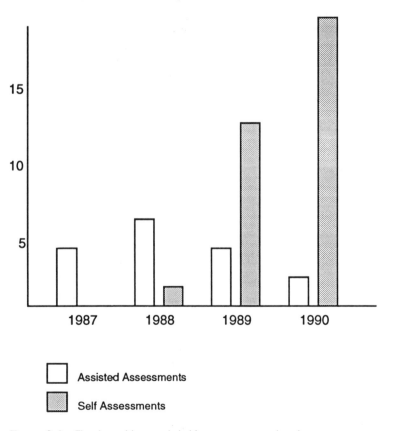

Figure 2.4   The trend towards taking process seriously

There are other signs that the process of software development is receiving considerable attention. Furthermore, international standards initiatives such as ISO-SPICE are focusing not just on installing a set of rules but on a framework which allows people to deliver continually improving quality in software products.

The current trend towards better defined and more flexible processes has a clear motivation as demonstrated in Figure 2.5 which illustrates the benefits over time recorded by one company after it initiated a software process improvement programme. After an initial rise in costs (for the installation and maintenance of a quality management system plus measurement and improvement project), the savings through less rework more than paid for the initial investment. The net effect after the first two years was to reduce overall project costs by some 15%.

There is now a significant body of evidence that show that quality costs but that mistakes cost more. Figure 2.5 illustrates the net saving for one company after the introduction of an improvement programme. Given this, reasonably valid returns on investment can be calculated to justify the introduction of a process improvement programme.

This is not the whole story, though. Just as a QMS can constrain more than it enables, so too can an improvement programme go wrong if it becomes an end in its own right. The people who produce the goods and the product they create need to be considered along with the process. There are fewer facts, figures and techniques to substantiate this but experience has shown over and again that a balance is essential for success.

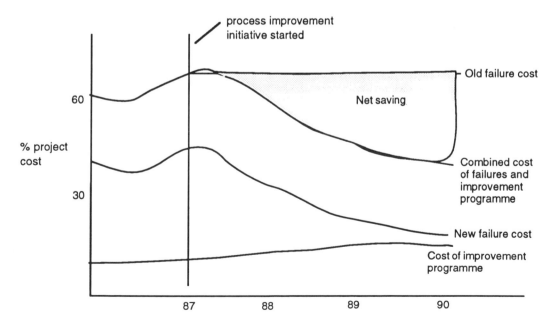

Figure 2.5   The cost of quality

The product

The difficulty of measuring software was illustrated with a simple example at the start of this chapter. It is easy to gather lots of data about software but very difficult to use it effectively.

The problem is not merely that few people agree what constitutes a line of code. A more fundamental issue is that there are few proven cause and effect links. For instance, if you have a 10 000 line program, is it more maintainable than a 5000 line program? How could you tell which one is the easier to update? How can you define a sensible set of measures that relate to what the customer wants?

On the one hand you have designs and code that can be characterised in terms of size, complexity, test coverage, information flow etc. On the other you have expectations in the form of reliability, flexibility, usability, etc. It is difficult to define a set of software measures that can be used as predictors of product quality.

The picture is not quite as downbeat as this: useful product measures are emerging and are explained in Chapter 5. Even so, in the absence of accepted or absolute measures, we need to look to experience, and there are some useful generalisations that we can make:

```
Total size                      10 Million statements
Number of major components      1000
Component size                  10,000 statements
Design life                     10 years
Project team                    100 engineers
Quality                         1 error/10,000 statements
Productivity                    50 statements/person/day
Rate of repair¹                 1 day/fault/1000 statements
```

Figure 2.6   Where are the limits?

The above figures aim to show roughly what is possible within 'state of the art' software projects. Average figures in most projects are an order of magnitude lower (e.g. an average project would have nearer 10 than 100 programmers, etc). Also, some figures vary with the type of application. For instance, the productivity figure of 50 statements/person/day depends on the level of language used, the amount of code reused, etc.

These figures are simply based on experience—and the more experience we get, the more currency such rules of thumb will carry. The size of software will always depend to some extent on your viewpoint—1 Mbyte is a

---

[1] This is a compound measure that gives the time to fix each fault for every 1000 statements of overall program size (e.g. the bigger the program, the longer it takes to fix a fault).

lot of data to enter, not much space when you are trying to fit a program into it—but meaningful metrics are emerging (see Appendix 2).

Despite the fact that the 'standard software metre' is yet to be established, the increasing accumulation of project data is beginning to yield significant correlations (e.g. between code size and its maintainability). The techniques outlined in Chapter 5 use these correlations to insert valid measurement points through the development path of the product.

The people

In many cases, the behaviour of the people working on a project gives the clearest pointer to its health. There are some typical behaviour patterns (such as the permanent firefighting team forever doing on-site patches, etc) that give a sure sign of a project in turmoil. Despite this, the people aspects of a successful project are often overlooked or, at least, treated as something separate from the project itself (e.g. 'support' roles such as personnel are often blamed if people are treated badly in the workplace).

Capable people who know what they are trying to achieve are essential to a healthy project. In fact, they are the most important single consideration. Figure 2.7, which shows the measured impact over a number of software projects of factors that contribute to productivity, substantiates this statement [Boe81].

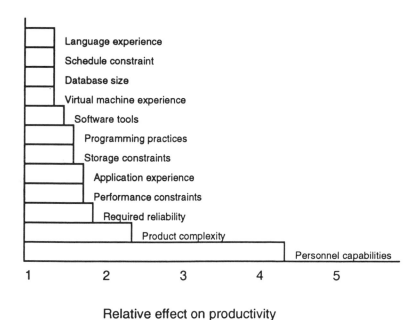

Relative effect on productivity

Figure 2.7   Where does productivity come from on software projects?

As well as being the most important factor, people are also the most complex and the most difficult to generalise about. It is not easy to prescribe solutions to deal with process and product issues but there are some rules. The people aspect of a healthy project is much more difficult to be conclusive about.

Nonetheless, there are some valid guidelines, some warning signs and some positive steps. The easiest of the guidelines is that the best way to improve productivity is to invest effort in the people who are involved in software projects. On the face of it, this statement is obvious to the point of naivety. In practice, though, one only has to look at the proportion of the software journals devoted to technical rather than people development to see that it receives a low priority.

Figure 2.8 shows the extent to which the gains in software development come from investment in people rather than in machines or new methods.

It is clear that, if improvements are to be made, the simple steps of informing and educating the people who contribute to the project need to be taken [Vra86]. This does not necessarily mean training everyone to use the latest design method. It *does* mean making those on the project more aware of their role and how they fulfil it.

This can be very simple to implement. For instance, a few years ago one of us delegated the task of copying disks for disaster backup on one software project to a clerk from a central support unit. Over a month passed before it was discovered that the disks had been religiously 'copied' at the end of every working day—and the *photo*copies had been duly locked in the fire-safe. A little time spent on 'knowledge growth' would have been most valuable in this instance!

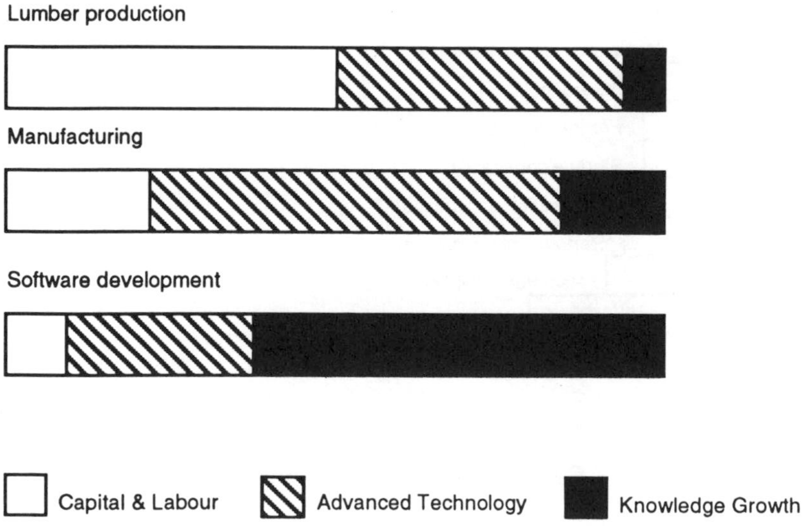

Figure 2.8 Where are gains to be made?

2.4 SUMMARY

This chapter has set the scene for the remainder of the book by explaining the special needs of software projects and how people, process and product can be addressed in that context.

Two factors that make software projects particularly difficult to successfully manage were discussed here. The first was that the detail of software matters. One mistake can make the difference between success and failure and it is difficult to state what is required with both clarity and precision.

The second factor is that the intangible nature of software make it *inherently* error prone. The customer rarely gets exactly what they think they asked for.

These two factors, together with the sheer complexity of modern systems, indicate that traditional engineering project management techniques are the base for software projects but that more needs to be added to ensure good health.

The three-P framework is developed in this chapter to show where attention should be focused within the project. In summary, this is:

● The product—setting appropriate targets and measures to get some handle on the status of what is being developed.

● The people—focusing individual and team capabilities onto the overall goals of the project.

● The process—setting up a controlled but enabling environment, the happy medium between anarchy and bureaucracy.

How and when to effect the above is the subject of the rest of the book.

REFERENCES

[ACA86] (1986) *Software—A Vital Key to UK Competitiveness* UK Cabinet Office report

[Boe81] Boehm B (1981) *Software Engineering Economics* (Prentice Hall 1988)

[Fre87] Freeman P (1987) *Software Perspectives* Addison Wesley

[Hob90] Hobday J (1990) Opening address *Software Engineering 90 Conference (Brighton, July 1990)*

[NR92] Norris M and Rigby P (1992) *Software Engineering Explained* John Wiley & Sons

[Vra86] Vrana C (1986) Education—the common denominator in solving the software crisis *Proc 6th Intl Software Engineering for Telecommunication Systems (Eindhoven, 1986)*

3

The Good, the Bad and the Average

*Projects don't slip a month at a time—
they slip an hour at a time*

John Martin

The term 'software crisis' was coined as far back as 1968 but the term crisis has subsequently proved to be rather misleading—the litany of software project failures since then indicates that the crisis is, in fact, an epidemic. In the UK alone, runaway software projects have cost billions of pounds. According to recent surveys of large project effectiveness, 62% of high technology companies suffer from at least one major failure over a five year period. More worrying is the finding that there is a 30% chance of any major software project becoming a runaway—and the larger the initial project budget, the more prone it is to overrun and overspend.

There are, however, many common causes of failed projects that would, if heeded, avoid painful repetition. There are early warning signs that can be used to initiate restorative action.

A few sought-after individuals have learned to recognise these signs and, in some cases, cure the ills that bedevil software projects. The software industry as a whole, though, has yet to reach the stage of maturity whereby it is standard practice to diagnose and treat these recurring problems. Examining some case studies for what goes wrong and why is a first step along the way to establishing some basis for progress.

This chapter gives an account of what happened on a few real projects—some good, others not so good. Although based on specific cases, the observations and lessons in this chapter are widely applicable. The names and dates on the projects may have been changed but the authors have had each one either claimed or disowned by numerous people.

To put things into perspective, we will first look at the very worst and best of projects before giving a more detailed example of a more representative software project.

3.1 THE BAD

Some projects go wrong by delivering late. Some fail to deliver what the customer wanted. Some simply cost too much. Truly spectacular failures manage to do all three by failing to deliver what was wanted, delivering it too late to be of any use and costing more than anyone was prepared to pay.

It may seem, at first sight, beyond belief that projects are allowed to carry on with unacceptable cost, time and quality. It does happen though and often with quite reasonable decisions being taken along the way.

Computerisation of the Health Service

In 1986, Guys Hospital in London was chosen by the UK Government as a showpiece for how modern technology should be used to manage complex resources. Over a million pounds worth of hardware and software was installed to provide computerised support for patient administration and records. Four years later the system was abandoned without ever having functioned satisfactorily. Within a year of this, another system called nCARE was installed. It was intended to provide similar facilities to the first system. It suffered a similar fate. In 1990 a third patient administration system called GIANT was installed—by 1992 it had not seen active service.

This series of unsuccessful attempts to put information technology into the Health Service is not unique. Over the last 10 years there have been many instances of systems that cost many millions of pounds to install. Most of them were scrapped or not put to effective use and there proved to be a number of common reasons behind all of the failures.

The first (and, perhaps, most telling) common theme was that all the systems had three, distinct groups who were involved in their introduction. There were the hospital's administrators, who wanted to have efficient, tightly run units. Then there were the computer consultants who offered a range of high technology solutions. Finally there were the users—the doctors and nurses who would be operating the systems. Rarely, if ever, did these three groups establish a consensus view of what could and should be provided. The end results reflected this lack of accord, with some of the main problems being:

- *Accuracy of data.* There was little motivation for the people who used the systems to enter data accurately. Since they were often not trained to use the technology, and nor could they see why the data was required, errors were often made in data entry. Moreover, since the transfer of information into the computer was seen as a pointless chore, it was often delegated to the hospital orderlies who had even less motivation to put accurate data into the systems.

- *Interpretation of data*. The data collected from each hospital was collated into a regional data set and then into a national data set. Along the way there were several instances where data had to be moved between different types of machines—sometimes this meant it had to be transferred by hand. Further errors were inevitably introduced to the already suspect data by the low level of compatibility across the various systems

- *Automation before analysis*. A key driver in the use of computerised systems was that it would support and speed the processing of patients through the hospital. In only a few cases was any analysis of the existing way of working carried out. More often than not, the systems were being introduced to support an ill-defined process.

- *Scale not recognised*. One of the most telling signs of the lack of end user involvement in the system planning was that the scale of the problems being tackled was often underestimated. In one instance, the required processing power was increased so much that the local electricity supply could not support the number of computers that had to be installed. Another proposed design was halted when it was realised that it would take of the order of 70 years to enter all the existing patient records into the new system, by which time they would be well past their useful life!

There are some fundamental reasons why things did not go to plan here. One of the main ones was the flux in system requirements. Much of the specification work for the systems was contracted out to external consultants. Each successive attempt at automation brought with it a different consultant with a different set of ideas on how the problem should be tackled. In the absence of a clear requirement definition process, there could be little consistency from one development to another.

A second key reason behind the system failures can be traced to a lack of analysis of the end user needs. As outlined above, the accuracy and interpretation of the data collected were both poor. The whole point of computerisation was to manage data, yet little attention was paid to *how* it would be collected, presented and interpreted. In pilot trials there was often a 100% (and greater) variance in costings for similar episodes between comparable hospitals. This should have triggered speedy re-evaluation of a key aspect of the system function. In practice, the users' view of the usefulness of the information was not taken into account.

At the end of the day, this was not a successful project. The customers were worse off both financially and in terms of the time wasted trying to work with an inappropriate system. The end users were frustrated by extra work for no perceived benefit. Perhaps some of the consultants who came, advised and left might have claimed success but even here the runaway nature of the overall project undermines this claim.

Sick projects do not always end up with the customer losing and the supplier winning. There are equally sick projects where the customer gets more than their fair share, at a cost to the supplier.

Process integration tool (PIT)

In order to exploit some successful research at a London university, a small venture company was started in the mid 1980's. The company aimed to provide consultancy based around a general purpose process automation tool that they had developed.

The tool itself was well ahead of its commercial competitors in that it was designed to allow special purpose application to be added through defined interfaces to a set of core facilities (e.g. regulated file access, process templates, etc) that provided all the basic functions.

The promise of the product was soon recognised. In particular, one of the large software houses was keen to use the product to control their own production procedures. It wasn't very long before the small venture company was spending 80% of its effort building the specific applications required by the large software house. Since some of these applications supported languages and procedures peculiar to the large company, a significant amount of time was spent working at the customer sites.

The first delivery of the system, PIT1, was a disappointment. It carried out the required functions but was far too slow for practical use. For instance, even the authors could type fast enough to overflow the buffer on the context sensitive editor. It was decided not to release the system for field trial. Both parties sat down to see how they could resolve the problems.

The only viable options were to optimise the generic tool applications or to integrate the special purpose routines more closely, ignoring the standard interfaces. Both options meant that the general purpose nature of the original product would have to be compromised. Nonetheless, by now this customer so dominated business that it was decided to go for close coupling of the special purpose applications.

After six months of rework, PIT2 was delivered. It was significantly faster than PIT1 and also had many added functions. PIT2 was released to three sites for trial. In the first month of the trial, no requests for change were received from two of the sites, but over 50 from the third. Investigation revealed that the core set of automated processes provided by PIT2 were already in place at the two sites that raised no change requests. They had exercised the system, found a few faults but had not seen PIT2 as a replacement for their existing processes. So it sat on the shelf, unused.

At the third site, there were few existing automated processes. Even so, the requests for change were clustered around two areas—the progress reporting module and the release management module. It became clear that these two functions were useful but PIT2, as an integrated set of tools, was not really a viable option in practice. The project was therefore cancelled at this point, some three years after the first meeting with the supplier.

The large software house was quite happy with the final outcome. They had acquired a set of tools that, even outside an integrated environment, were to prove useful. Also, the close working relationship with a team of people whose ideas were at the forefront of technology led to a significant influx of new ideas.

On this occasion, though, the supplier lost. They became so tied to one customer that they were less able to deliver after the project than they had been beforehand. This was not an inevitable conclusion and there were a number of early warning signs that could, if heeded, have led to a more successful conclusion. Several of the people in the supplier team saw the dominance of one customer as a problem—this manifested itself in uncertainty over whether local management or the customer were in charge. Some time invested in risk assessment may well have picked up this, and other signs.

3.2 THE GOOD

There are some projects where both customer and supplier were better off afterwards. The former was left with something useful, that worked for reasonable cost. The latter had built up good experience and had at least one willing customer for the future. The literature is not overburdened with these stories of success but here is one, for illustration.

Telephone payment checking

This project had a fairly unpromising start. As part of a reorganisation, several people had to move between two software development offices quite quickly. In the ensuing rush, no-one remembered to pay the phone bill and the reminder bill, routinely sent a week before disconnection, was not found until it was too late! The experience of having to recover the situation along with all the other fuss and bother of the move triggered a thought in the minds of those affected—how best to prevent this happening again.

The fact that those concerned worked closely with the local telephone district meant that this was more than an idle thought. Within a few weeks of the incident an outline proposal had been put together for a telephone payment checking system.

The aim of the system was simple—to maximise the number of outstanding reminder bills that get paid. After a period of negotiation, both sides were happy with the proposal and a short requirements specification was drawn up. This stipulated that the system should take information from the existing telephone customer database, sort the outstanding bills by size and time unpaid and maximise the daily number of customers contacted.

The first thoughts of the design team were to use as much technology as possible in the solution. A design emerged that did everything automatically. It interfaced directly to the telephone customer database, sorted all those to be reminded into a priority order, downloaded this list into a message sending device and finally logged the day's results. On the face of it, this fulfilled all of the stated requirements … and would be great fun to work on, too. An outline of the initial systems is illustrated in Figure 3.1.

At this stage, though, some very fundamental questions started to go through the team's mind: how will we know if the message sender has really made contact? what if a child answers? or an answerphone?

Doubts over the wisdom of doing it all with technology soon spread and it emerged that the volume of calls would require a huge investment in message senders. Also, the interface to the main telephone customer database looked like being a more complex and costly development than it had first appeared. The only thing to do at this point was to go and look at the existing arrangement to find ways round the problem.

Then a new light dawned. Armed with an appreciation of the current situation and of what could be done, it became clear how to proceed. A re-examination of the original aim of the system confirmed that the requirements could all be met despite the technical problems.

It transpired that there was no real need to take information off the telephone customer database—it could be processed into priority order before being presented to the operators. This simple change had a dramatic effect on the rate at which the operators could clear reminder calls. And the problem of whether the message had really got through didn't arise with the human operators still part of the system. The actual design in this project (Figure 3.2) was considerably different to the original thoughts.

The focus of the project continued to swing away from an isolated, technical solution to one of optimising the existing situation. A brief analysis of how

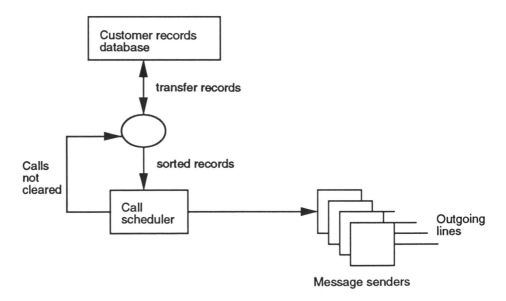

Figure 3.1 The first attempt at the payment checking system

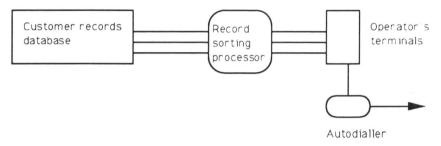

Figure 3.2   The eventual system configuration

the operators spent their time revealed that a considerable amount was spent dialling numbers. An enhancement to the system was put together that dialled a customer's number as their database record went up on the operator's screen. A final enhancement allowed the operators to record the result of each call directly on the customer record so that it could be re-prioritised for a further call or returned for storage.

By the end of the project, everyone involved was better off. The operators had been equipped to do their job more efficiently, the successful clear rate for outstanding debts shot up and the software project team were content with a job well done. And with their increased ability to provide solutions, not just technology.

Why did this project go so well? The main reasons were:

- The main thing was kept the main thing. The project team never lost sight of their objective. They could easily have been seduced by 'clever' solutions—the use of message senders, smart software to detect answerphones, etc. They continually asked the question 'will this clear more unpaid accounts?'

- The overall system was kept in view. Ideas were tested against how they would work in a national implementation. This revealed very clear preferred solutions. For instance, the idea that there should, for economy, be a centralised reminder service was rejected when the volume of long distance calls per day was calculated!

- Early wins. Delivery was phased to provide small improvements at regular intervals. Both customer and supplier could see that the project was moving forward.

- User involvement. The effects of the proposed solution were tested on the end user as soon as was practical. This was invaluable in revealing how the user would *actually* use the system (rather than how they were supposed to). For instance, in a similar project, the first time headsets were introduced to enable hands-free operation in a dealing room, the project team found that everyone started throwing pieces of paper at each other to attract attention. It was not at all obvious that, in practice, they were talking to each other as well as down two phones.

3.3   THE AVERAGE

The bulk of software projects fall somewhere between the examples given above. Even so, they can be characterised to some extent and the more common problem areas can be highlighted.

A field information system

In the early days of computerisation, many small systems were installed to handle local procedures more efficiently than the manual systems they replaced. This was certainly the case in this example where a number of pay and personnel records systems, installed across the UK 10 years previously, were still doing an effective job.

There was a need for change, though. The user base served by the installed systems had changed considerably since they were first commissioned. There was greater need for data to be compiled across systems and the required loadings and response times were outgrowing the existing capacity.

The project to replace the variety of stand alone systems with a new, integrated system began quite well. A project team was established with representatives from the users (who operated the existing systems), the sponsors (the central finance and personnel authorities) and the developers of the new system.

After a couple of months this team had produced a statement of requirements (SOR) for the new integrated pay and personnel records system. The project, christened NIPPER by the team, now had to be formally approved—first by the internal investment committee and then by the systems architecture board—before the development could start.

The formal SOR review with the internal investment committee went smoothly. The basic need for the system was agreed and the SOR was approved subject to a few additions. These additions were largely focused on the provision of collated statistics from the local nodes. The consequence of this was that the central node (originally envisaged as a small system element) would now be carrying out a significant amount of processing on large volumes of data. Nonetheless, the project team were happy that the basic structure and function of NIPPER were intact.

At the review with the systems architecture board no changes were made to the structure of NIPPER. Some decisions on allocation of responsibilities were, however, made. Due to the diversity of physical size of each area and types of operation they carried out, it was decided that each should be responsible for its own part of the development. This meant there would be three sub-systems. The central system node would be the responsibility of corporate finance and personnel.

The initial misgivings of the team were allayed by the suggestion that there would be a central design team responsible for setting development standards to be used by all of the sub-systems.

Timescales for NIPPER had become quite pressing by the time it emerged from this second review, so the design work was started immediately afterwards. While the central team set out technical and procedural standards, the various area developments were busy planning and specifying their sub-systems. Progress was rapid and within six months the design teams met for the first of two critical design reviews (CDR)

The input to the CDR was some 600 pages of text and diagrams describing the plans and structure of the four elements of NIPPER. The review was attended by the team that generated the original SOR, the current development teams and finance and personnel representatives. After about six hours of presentations, questions and observations the plans and designs were accepted. Everyone was happy that it would all work and that issues such as backup, installation, performance and operation had been adequately catered for.

Following the review, everything went to plan. Despite some problems with incompatible compilers, the coding and testing of the sub-systems was completed to schedule. The first major slip was encountered in integration testing. Despite the standards set and imposed by the central team, the data presented to the central node by the sub-systems proved to be very variable. Small discrepancies, such as the format of information (e.g. three different date formats were used) and the order of messages, proved to be difficult both to trace and to fix.

All of a sudden, the project started to free fall. Having been on schedule for over a year, it was slipping day by day. Once design errors were unearthed during integration testing, the main problem was to understand how the system elements worked at all! Subtle differences in the approaches of the central and area teams became apparent—different versions of software were being used from one team to another, naming conventions were far from standard, sometimes data was embedded in the program, sometimes not etc etc.

It was nearly eight months before all of these problems were rectified—double the original. The knock-on effect of the extra time and effort required to recover the situation was that the planned time for user training and installation was lost. Perhaps worse was the fact that no-one was really sure what the delivered documentation actually referred to.

NIPPER was finally released about four months late. Despite some teething troubles (mostly its inability to drive some of the area printers), it performed to the original requirements. The team designated to maintain the system (none of whom had developed it) had significant problems in the first few months but did manage to establish some control thereafter. Their only worry was that they knew the performance of the system was lacking and were worried at the prospect of reworking some of the more 'spaghetti'-like parts of the system.

Overall, the project was viewed as a reasonably successful one, on the grounds that it met the original requirements. The system was extended to serve seven more areas over the next four years. Diversity of local procedures meant that each new area was treated as a separate development and each required some changes to be made to the central system. The option of extending the functionality of NIPPER was never mentioned again.

As with the other projects, there are a number of factors that were, in retrospect, key to the final outcome. In the case of the NIPPER project these were:

- *The early system configuration choice.* The real consequences of splitting the development on organisational grounds were not really thought through. In some ways the decision made sense, as each part of the development was placed with those who best understood the local requirements. The negative factor that could have been addressed early on was the creation of local variants. The option of partitioning the system into common and local modules was never considered. Consequently, the development of common code which could be configured with different sets of initialisation data was not on the plan. In reality, a considerable amount of maintenance effort was required to support all the system variants.

- *Interfaces.* Despite the fact that the interfaces between the systems were defined, there was no common design team to implement them. Each team worked to the interface specifications: problems with interpretation were not found until integration testing. A little extra early effort in setting up a common design team to implement the system interfaces would have allowed sharing of code and documentation and would probably have saved time and effort in the long run.

- *Coordination between teams.* Once the development phase was complete, NIPPER was handed over to be maintained by a completely separate team. The maintenance team had played no part in the system design or implementation. Quite apart from having to learn how the system worked with little inside knowledge, the maintenance team found that NIPPER had been designed to work to its original requirement. It had not been designed to evolve to cope with the demands placed on the system by its users

- *Critical design reviews.* The importance of the first critical design review was not fully appreciated. This review effectively set the overall framework for the system development. Yet it was treated more as a set of presentations and proposals than an analysis of how best to meet the stated requirement. It is significant (and typical) that the review was attended by more resource and financial managers than analysts. Yet the decisions taken were essentially technical. Spurious problems were raised (e.g. on security features) that knocked on into unnecessary design complications

- *Important problems lost in the confusion.* The problems found during integration testing could have been found earlier in the project if simple monitoring had been in place. The project controls used here were purely cost and schedule ones. It appeared that all was going well in the early stages because replans simply curtailed original allowances for testing. Also, there was one key system component which, if identified early, could have been put on the critical path (in the event, it was one of the last to be scheduled into integration tests). Had the complexity of each system module been plotted against its size (and this data was available) then a map similar to Figure 3.3 would have been the result. This shows two 'outliers': A and B. One of them (B) was a keyboard scanning routine which was intrinsically complex. The other outlier (A) was simply written in a very convoluted way. Early sight of this fact would have saved a lot of time in both test and maintenance!

Specific projects are useful to illustrate points but each one is different. Before moving on to what symptoms to look for and what remedies to consider, it is possible to generalise about software projects. There are some gross statements that do apply time and again [Leh80]—some laws of software projects.

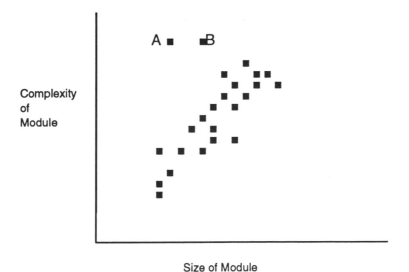

Figure 3.3   Outlying modules

3.4   GENERAL OBSERVATIONS ON SOFTWARE PROJECTS

Some of the problems encountered in the above stories occur over and over again. This section aims to outline where the project norms are, in much the same way that Figure 2.6 gave some approximate limits on our technical capabilities for software production.

Project stages

In principle software projects follow some sort of process—usually called a 'lifecycle' [Ago88]. Requirements are captured and analysed before design gets under way; the product is tested before release. There are many different types of lifecycle [KF81] but they all focus on the technical aspects of the project. When we look at where the time goes in projects, we get a different sort of picture. Figure 3.4 shows the typical allocation of time, based on the experience of several hundred developments, as a project moves from its initial, broad concept to its final, precise implementation. It indicates that the technical aspects of software projects that have received considerable attention over the years are but one part of the overall picture.

On any sizeable project a considerable proportion of time and effort is spent finding out what *really* needs to be done, who needs to do it and by when. This phase can be called requirements capture, politics or even waiting for inspiration. Whatever it is called, it does happen (e.g. much the first

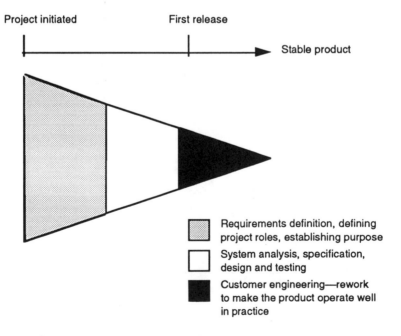

Figure 3.4   Where project time really goes

part of the NIPPER project was concerned with allocation of tasks) and needs to be understood. The figure is broad at this point to reflect the range of options that are open in this phase. Since a common view of what the project should be focused on is key here, attention to the people issues is crucial. The typical split of activity[1] in this phase is:

40%—establishing the scope of the project.
35%—defining exactly what the need is
25%—writing a business case.
10%—establishing and analysing a formal statement of requirements

It is this first part of the project that should set a clear overall purpose—a whole life rationale [RN90] This, in turn, allows those that have to work on the project to exercise sensible judgement during its development. Also it is at this stage that the structure of the project is set up arbitrary decisions (such as going for multi-site working) taken early in a project can multiply problems later on.

The middle part of Figure 3.4 is the best understood portion and there are numerous tools, methods and techniques available to help here [NCC87]. A typical split of activity here is:

20%—specification and design
20%—prototyping and testing of ideas
30%—implementation
30%—test and rework.

The 'customer engineering' portion of Figure 3.4 is again ill-covered by conventional theory. The problem is different to the first phase—it is now clear where the target is but it is difficult to meet the precise end result. Typical activities in this area are rework of the product to make it go fast enough, and provision of extra documentation to make it maintainable and usable. Approximate times in this phase are:

25%—installation testing
50%—re-engineering for acceptable field performance
15%—adding essential user features not in original specification
10%—supplementary information for maintenance.

It should be noted that the above reflects what really goes on—not necessarily what should happen. This will be revisited later on.

Real and imagined productivity

We have already discussed the lack of absolute measures for software. Given this, it is very difficult to put forward any meaningful definition of productivity on software projects. Whatever it *is* defined to be, there are some things that it definitely is not. These spurious signals need to be recognised.

---

[1] These activities are not necessarily sequential.

On the face of it, all of the projects described here were well controlled—plans were in place, support documentation was written. The common thread in what went wrong can be traced back to the three Ps, introduced in Chapter 1. The process (the vehicle for assessing progress) was not linked to the people (who were responsible for causing progress).

Typical instances of this are intermediate measures (such as monthly '% project related activity' targets) that do not actually relate to the end target. It is important to differentiate action from progress. Operational and intermediate targets are useful planning aids and they give confidence but they are empty milestones if they are not related directly to end product delivery. The empty milestones often make the most noise because they are the easiest ones to set and to measure.

In the absence of any hard metrics, it is very easy to place emphasis on the figures that can be generated from an installed process. These figures should not be ignored but they can mislead more than they enlighten, especially if taken on their own.

After one audit, on a project run to very tight timescales, one of the development team observed that the auditors' role was to go around after the war and shoot the wounded: the customer was happy with the product, the team were proud of their work yet the figures being used by local management showed the project to be a poor performer.

Comparisons

It is often assumed that improved tools and methods will make a project better. There is little evidence to support this—in fact, there are many pointers to the fact that as long as the basic needs of communication[2] and essential automation[3] are satisfied, further technology support has only a marginal effect.

International comparisons between US, UK and Japanese software projects shed a little more light on this. These indicate very little difference in relative abilities to produce systems of comparable size and quality to the same timescales. The only two areas that do emerge as sources of competitive advantage are the quality of design and the level of reuse. Both of these are people dependent—the former on individuals, the latter on shared culture (Japanese developers seem more disposed to sharing than those in the US or UK).

The clear indication is that extra equipment does not really solve problems. Put this together with Brooks' observation that more people thrown at a project usually slow it down rather than speed it up [Bro87] and the need to carefully manage the three Ps is clear.

---

[2] This encompasses infrastructure for electronic mail, document preparation and printing, etc.

[3] Compilers, debuggers, regression test equipment, etc.

Trends and Expectations

Finally, a few trends in, and expectations of, software projects.

It is virtually impossible to predict the future. Even so as a general rule, we tend to overestimate what will happen in the next two years and underestimate what will happen in the next ten. In 10 years a likely situation is that:

- *Processor speeds*. The personal computer in the high street shop today is more powerful than the average mainframe a decade ago. Over the next decade, that sort of progress could well be repeated.

- *Storage*. Data storage costs have fallen by several orders of magnitude over the last ten years. The cost of storage in the next century will be nearly zero.

- *Complexity*. Figure 3.5. shows the growth in complexity of aerospace systems software. The story is no different for network and telecommunications software. If this continues for the next decade, there will be billions of lines of code in operation, being maintained.

- *Speed*. It used to be acceptable for screens to remain blank for several seconds while the software went though its calculation. Future systems will be expected to react immediately.

- *Quality*. Ten years ago software was expected to fall over the first time it was installed. Current systems are not perfect but they are expected to work. In ten years software will have to work first time, every time.

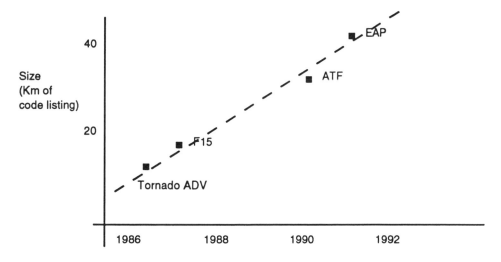

Figure 3.5   The growing complexity of software systems

- *Integration*. Despite the accelerating use of software-based systems, it is still difficult to share information, components and applications between systems. Over the next ten years, users will expect to have consistent access to a wide range of processing engines and information sources— from one terminal, quickly, with security.

3.5 SUMMARY

Much of the information in this book is obvious. Yet the same mistakes are made over and over again in software projects. Part of the reason for this is that it is one thing to know how to do something in theory, another to experience it first hand.

This chapter goes some way to laying out a point of practical reference for the rest of the book by describing some real projects. In each case, there were some basic decisions—some good, some bad—that impacted on the outcome of the project.

It is easier to remember guidelines when they are related to reality and that is what this chapter has tried to provide. From this point on we look in some detail at the symptom that can be used to spot a sick project.

Note added in proof

Do we learn from our mistakes? A few weeks after this book was completed, yet another major software project died. If some of the signs of ill-health had been recognised, could it have been saved? Consider some of the quotes from those involved.

'The seeds of failure were sown in 1989'

'I don't think anyone understood the whole project'

'With hindsight we were trying to satisfy too many interests'

'We never stood back and said, "what would be the most sensible way of building this system"'

'It was always going to be delayed three months. Never a few days, never a week, always three months......that seemed enough time to put things right'

'They were still specifying the operational requirements when they started testing'

'They said it couldn't be done in the time-scale—they didn'y say it hadn't even been started'

'No-one was brave enough to stand up and say this doesn't make sense'

and the final quote from one of the articles was.

'It could happen again and will happen again'

Paraphrasing Oscar Wilde, to lose one project is careless, to lose another the same way is negligent. There is plenty still to be learnt from other people's mistakes. And it's cheaper and healthier than making your own.

(All quotes are taken from The Financial Times (19/3/93) or The Independent (14/3/93))

REFERENCES

[Ago88] Agostoni G *et al* (1988) Managing software quality during the complete lifecycle *First European Seminar on Software Quality (Brussels, 1988)*

[Bro87] Brooks F (1990) No silver bullet *IEEE Software*, April 1990

[KF81] Kerola P and Freeman P (1981) A comparison of life cycle models *Proc. 5th Int. Conf. on Software Engineering (San Diego, 1981)*

[Leh80] Lehman M (1980) Programs, lifecycles and laws of software evolution *Proc. IEEE* pp 1060–1076

[NCC87] National Computer Centre/Dept. of Trade and Industry (1987) *The STARTS Guide—a Guide to Software Methods and Tools* pp44-59 1987

[RN90] Rigby P and Norris M (1990) The software death cycle *Proc. UK IT 90 Conference (March 1990)*

[Bro87] Brooks F (1990) No silver bullet: essence and accidents of software engineering *Computer* vol 20 no 4

4

Symptoms

Forewarned is forearmed

Royal Observer Corps Motto

In the previous chapters we have described what happened on a number of software projects—some good and some bad. Given that it is easy to be wise in hindsight, a number of general observations could readily be made about these projects. But it is important to remember that not all the people involved with a project will have the same viewpoint. Different people will see different things as the project proceeds. And what is seen by the developers as a successful project may not necessarily be seen as a good project by the customer or end user.

The problem with the judgement of good or bad is that it is usually takes place at the end of the project or, worse, when the project is stopped due to problems. At this stage it is very expensive if not impossible to correct a sick project, as the market window has passed by or the budget has been consumed. Therefore we need to be able to spot the symptoms of projects that have the problems. The earlier this is done the better.

The main focus of this chapter is to identify some indicators or measures of the project symptoms that we can apply to the project at an early stage. These indicators can be either hard or soft and different indicators will be relevant to different people. The hard measures can be project management data or errors per module, etc. Experience has shown that the soft measures of perceptions, feelings and team morale often give a better indication of the project's health than the hard ones.

4.1   CAN YOU MEASURE THE SICKNESS OR HEALTH OF A PROJECT?

Why do you diagnose symptoms of a sick project? In practice it is usually because you feel there are problems, but are not sure of the cause—rather like visiting the doctor when you feel ill. The doctor asks a series of questions to find the area of the problem. In effect, the doctor is attempting to find the systems that the symptoms indicate the problem is in, such as the renal, epidermal, etc, before applying the diagnostic technique to try and isolate the problem. Diagnostic techniques are usually applied before laying hands on the patent.

The process used is very formal and allows the doctor to reduce the many possibilities of the cause of the illness down to a manageable set of symptoms: at this point the hunt for the real problem starts. The first stage can be seen as assessing the look and feel of the patient. This process can be applied by analogy to software engineering—the sick projects you can tell by look and feel just by looking for the symptoms.

But what diagnostic techniques do we have to find the real problems of software projects?

One of the problems with software is that it cannot talk back to you and directly offer any help. But there are indicators and pointers to problem areas in projects. And that is what this chapter is all about.

First, some background to the difficulty of measuring the health of software projects and why we need to treat the symptoms early. The medical analogy of the doctor can be extended to the other software specialists and ancillary trades, including software geriatricians and undertakers to deal with the old and technically dead project. We know software will not wear out but its slow death will be costly for all concerned—customer, supplier, distributor, etc. From research in the USA and UK software maintenance can cost over 70% of total lifecycle costs; see Figure 4.1 which shows the amount consumed in the maintenance phase, old age and eventual death of a project [RN90]. There should be an active decision to kill or cure the project and this is covered in detail in Chapter 6. For now, we assume that the project is continuing and is ready for examination. So where do we start?

We have, as yet, no universally agreed measures of the goodness of the software produced by a project. We cannot directly measure goodness or quality. This is not surprising since there are no universally agreed size measures for software.

What have we got? There is evidence that if an error is discovered during design it will cost one monetary unit to correct. Relative to this cost the same error discovered just before testing will cost 6.5 units. During testing it will cost 15 units to fix and after testing it costs 65 units to correct [Pre88]. If you multiply the cost per bug by the number of bugs still in the system you reach the conclusion: *get them early and get as many as you can*. Figure 4.2 illustrates the point.

But how do you identify the sick project early enough to stop the inevitable disaster that will follow? By using diagnostic techniques on the project.

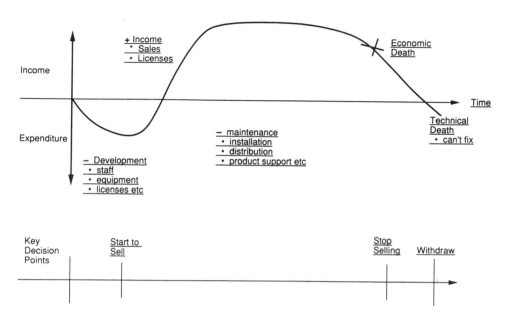

Figure 4.1 Software death cycle

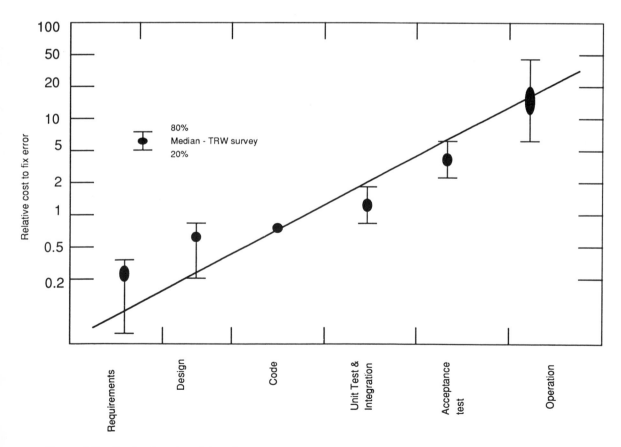

Figure 4.2 Costs of curing sick software

4.2   HOW TO IDENTIFY THE SICK PROJECT EARLY

The need to identify sick projects early has in the past concentrated on measures against project schedule plans, financial management and, to a much lesser extent, quality management systems. These practices will produce hard measures that have traditionally been used to manage and control projects. But as we said earlier the soft measures are as, if not more, important. They are a better indicator to the real health of the project.

Software projects are considered here as consisting of three main constituents, People, Process and Product [NR92], as outlined earlier. To identify the state of a project you need to start looking at some aspect of each of the three Ps simultaneously.

There has been a considerable amount of effort in looking at the process and attempting to measure the product but much less effort in the people areas. Yet there is considerable evidence [DML87] that you get the best quality software by using the best people and keeping them. Also a report by Posner lists the main reasons that IT projects fail [Pos87] and these are listed in Figure 4.3.

```
Inadequate resource      69%
Unrealistic deadlines    67%
Unclear direction        63%
Uncommitted team         59%
Insufficient planning    56%
Changes in direction     42%
Conflict between teams   35%
```

Figure 4.3   Why projects fail

If you analyse the list it comes down to poor communication as the basic underlying cause of the problems. There a number of questions that should be asked of the project managers—especially when it is remembered that they are the ones who produced most of the above list!

- If the resources were inadequate why did they not ask for more at the beginning or during the project?

- If the deadlines were unrealistic did they try to get them changed or even communicate the problem?

- If there were unclear goals or direction, who was setting them and was the problem communicated?

- If the team was too small to do the job and did not know what they had to produce or by when, is it any surprise they were uncommitted?

- Insufficient planning is self-evident from the first three as is the breakdown in communications and hence the conflict between departments.

- The change in goals and direction is part of the second symptom of project failure, and, if added, makes this the major problem.

The interesting thing about the list in Figure 4.2 is that project management itself was not seen as a problem. In fact the only people-related problem was the uncommitted team. Maybe it is the old medical saying 'physician heal thy self' that should be applied to the project managers who supplied this information. Either way it should give all project managers food for thought.

One cure for the above is to use Kipling's six honest serving men, by asking the why, what, where, when, who and how of the project. Communications is a problem with single site working but we are now developing systems on multiple sites, often using the new and untried tools of the computer network without any real understanding how this will affect the communications within the project.

Given this background, we will (rather like the doctor with his initial diagnosis) start to break the problem down into its three main systems—the people, the process and the product, or the three Ps of software.

4.3 HOW HEALTHY IS THE PROCESS?

The problem with Process Control or Management is that it is totally logical to have these in place. Anything that is totally logical is just common sense and must either exist or it must be simple to put in place. Therefore returning to our medical analogy, why are we not all jogging, eating a fat free diet and not eating meat or smoking? The answer is that it is not always human nature to do what is good for us—it hard to change the habits of a lifetime even if it is common sense.

Experience suggests, unfortunately, that one of the rarest commodities is mutually agreed common sense.

So, from the manager's perspective, why go to the expense of putting in a process or quality management system when it is usually the first thing abandoned in a crisis. Rather, like the diet, it is usually abandoned in a time of stress, The rule with poor software engineering is: *when the going gets tough, abandon the process.* And the abandonment of an established process is a sure indicator of project problems.

The reasons for abandoning a defined process are usually couched in different terms from the above. Some actual examples, which are symptoms of a project either in or heading for trouble, are listed below.

- We haven't the time to test it; ship it and we will sort the fault reports from the customer.

- This software is just for testing and the customer will not see it and hence we do not need to fully test it.

- When the process is wrong, or not designed with people, or the project's critical success factors in mind. The main thing is to keep the main thing as the main thing, i.e. make sure that we focus on doing this for the business and not just for the sake of the process.

- When the process police (the quality team, the project office or the programme team, etc) do not communicate effectively with the project teams.

- The inflexible process 'we have always done it this way and no one has ever complained so why should we change?'

- Empty milestones make the most noise. This is when you are hit by the process police for not delivering something that is not wanted or needed by the rest of the real project, just because it happens to be on the plan.

- When no-one can really explain the birth to death process of the project. It is not clear how the project delivers or who is responsible if it doesn't.

- Where no meaningful process measures are collected. No-one really knows where the project is.

- The never-updated plan and its partner, the plan that is rescheduled to make the actuals meet the predicted. Never trust a project that, according to the plan, has no problems.

4.4 HOW HEALTHY ARE THE PRODUCTS?

The identification of warning signs of a sick project in the product area is more difficult as there are few tangible product deliverables early in the life-cycle. Some of the best indicators are:

- The interim release followed by the onsite testing and debug. If this is scheduled in over a weekend, look very closely.

- Have you solved the business problem with the minimum effort? The object is to supply an acceptable solution at minimum cost beware the 'elegant solution'; this usually hides programming for programming's sake.

- Do you know what product you have got and where its relatives can be found? Poor configuration management is a project killer.

- Is the documentation appropriate to the product? No documentation may be acceptable in some cases but too much is definitely bad news. (Atomic submarines went to sea with six tons of documentation on board.)

Help is on the way, there are some useful techniques outlined in the next chapter that help. Even so, this is as yet an immature area.

4.5   HOW INVOLVED IN THE PROJECT ARE THE PEOPLE?

The people involved in the project will include the customer, the users, the management and the team. The team includes developers, testers and support—in fact, anyone who is directly involved with the process and development of the products.

Of the three Ps, people are the most complex. Why this is so can be difficult to understand as they can communicate, complain and kick up a fuss whereas with a process or product there is little active feedback. It may be, though, that despite lots of meetings, memos and presentations, poor *effective* communication is the major problem in software engineering.

It is generally accepted that poor staff with a good process will produce a poor product and that good staff with a poor (or non-existent) process can produce a good product. This is true in spite of management (and, often, to spite management).

A general rule that seems to hold with people is: when things go wrong either *blame the people* (management and customer's view) or *abandon the project* (the team view). For a project to be in good health, this polarisation has to be countered.

The people aspect of software engineering projects are further complicated as they can be considered from three totally different viewpoints—those of the team, the management and the customers. Each one needs to be considered carefully:

The team

Three of the giveaway signs of an unhealthy project at the workface are:

- a high percentage of staff turnover

- sick leave above the average number of days per year.

- people who do not know how they add value or contribute to the overall project objectives.

There will usually be a predominantly cynical attitude to the work and the management. This, at first sight, may not appear to be a major problem but this is where you can make your major gains in productivity and quality [DML87].

When looking at the health of a project from the people point of view, it is often informative to look for the use of different words for the same thing. When it's you it is resignation, sick leave or a nervous breakdown but to higher management it's attrition or the losses you suffer in a war.

One classic indicator of underlying problems is how the name of an issue changes as you go up the hierarchy of an organisation. The programmer has a Problem, which when passed up the tree becomes an Opportunity and eventually a Challenge. This, at first sight, is amusing but it hides a lack of communication and genuine interest in the people who work on the projects (see Figure 4.4)

The programmer has a problem and he owns it . As you go up the tree, the opportunity discussed by middle management is again owned by the programmer and when escalated (and, at the same time, usually emasculated) it arrives as a opportunity with the gods on Mount Olympus. Unfortunately the problem is still owned by the programmer.

The reaction at the workface is that if you get any more challenges from on high, then you will end up with this programmer retiring from the project either mentally or physically.

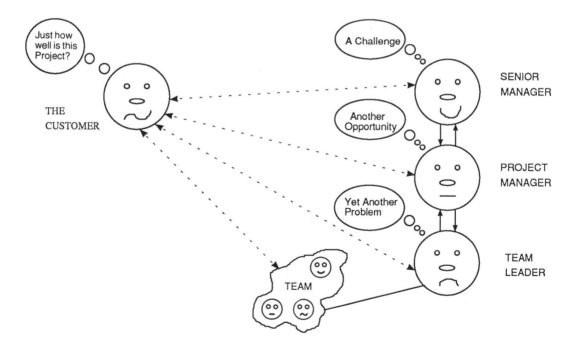

Figure 4.4   The different viewpoints of a project

The management

A frequent attitude among the managers of software projects is to boast about the amount of free overtime their staff work. In reality there is no such thing as free prolonged overtime—it is always accompanied by undertime [Pet85] or staff attrition.

Project managers should be concerned with staff turnover, divorce and sick leave. These are valid indicators as to how well the team is being managed. Having had the experience of losing a member of our teams, with no warning, due to them being unable to take the pressure, we can assure you it happens very easily and the time and effort to rectify the situation can be tremendous. There are usually indicators but spotting them can be difficult. Spotting them is impossible, though, if you are not looking for them.

The customer

All individual customers will have some preconceived ideas of what are the main requirements of the product or service being developed for them and will have a personal view of what they should be doing to ensure that the project achieves their personal ambitions. These ambitions may be in terms of time to deliver, cost and the features (or even the quality) of the final product.

The customer's concerns will be based upon individual exposure and previous experience of software development projects. These viewpoints can be seen as a series of levels of customer maturity which are dependent upon both the customers and developers experience of and exposure to dealing with the main issues.

The four levels are:

- *Initial*. Little or no previous experience, content to allow the 'professional software developers' to run the project and believe that the result will be an end product that has the functionality they want on time and to budget. The initial customer viewpoint can be described by the typical statement 'I know what I think I want.'

- *Concerned*. Some previous exposure, may have had a bad experience but not sure how to improve the situation. These customers are reluctant to be bitten again. They usually see external suppliers as better than internal just because they are external. Their viewpoint will be 'it is better to employ an external consultant than risk any more problems.'

- *Over-involved*. These customers have climbed the learning curve; they now strongly believe that they know best how to manage the project. They seek to do the project management at a distance. In short their viewpoint is 'I know what I want and need it today (or yesterday).' By this stage of their own development they also think they know how to get it. They usually show great dynamism and commitment, but will often start to accuse other people of lack of commitment to them or to the project when it starts to become sick.

- *Mature.* These customers have evolved through the previous levels and understand what to look for, accept their role and the contribution they have to make and can be summed up by the statement 'I think I know what I want and we will work on it together to produce it.'

There is a further problem prevalent in the software engineering industry. While customers can be classified into these four different types they can complicate matters by changing any stage, or maturing throughout the project. To manage these different types of customer you need to use different techniques and also different processes—see Figure 4.5.

For the *initial* type of customer you need to use the Technical Design-Centred approach where the framework of the project is presented to the customer to ensure they are informed and consulted throughout the design process. They are then in a position to commission and (somewhat later on) accept the system.

For *concerned* customers the joint customer/specialist process must be used. Here the user's representative(s) are involved in all the phases of the design. The risks involved in the project should be communicated at all stages to help ease any of their concerns.

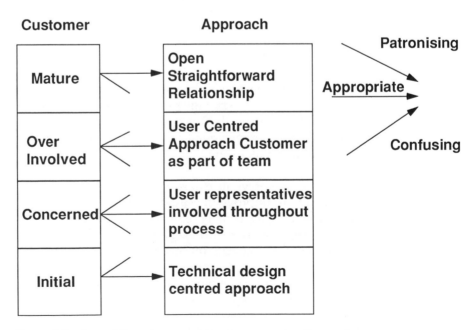

Figure 4.5   Four different approaches to managing the customer

With the *over-involved* type of customer it is necessary to adopt a User-Centred Design Approach, where the technical experts from the customer are be involved in (and contribute to) the design. Sometimes, they may even be part of the design team. This customer should be part of the risk analysis team and the earlier this can take place the better—if possible at the requirements stage. The object is to agree all the requirements before you start. This may not be possible, however, if state of the art or market critical software is being put together.

If at the start of the project all the requirements are not known this should be brought out in to the open by getting the customer to prioritise then review and re-review until a workable set of requirements can be agreed. A useful metric in this case is the number of urgent fax messages you find on your desk from the customer each week. Over ten and you have a psychotic customer—and real problems. The key with this type of customer is to get them involved as part of the process so that they know the real state of the project and can help plan, rather than continually react.

With the *mature* type of customer you ask for a specification of the approach they require from you, as the supplier, at the inception of the project. With this type of customer you should be looking for involvement in process improvement and the building of an open and honest relationship.

If you attempt to use the same approach to all your customers you are asking for trouble ... and you will get it. Figure 4.6 outlines the quality responsibilities.

This is not new information but perhaps it should be on the team, management and customer's wall. We outline the problems now for some classical early warning signs.

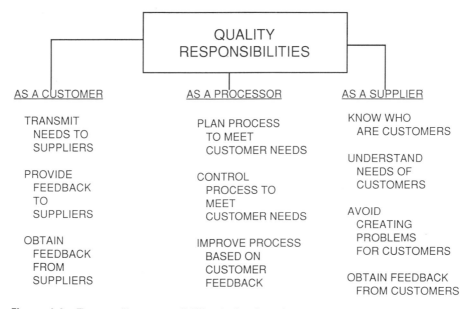

Figure 4.6 The quality responsibilities (after Juran)

4.6 CLASSIC EARLY WARNING SIGNS OF PEOPLE PROBLEMS

These are again listed from three viewpoints:

- the project manager
- the team
- the customer.

From the project manager's viewpoint there are a number of easily detected signs of a disaffected team. Some of the classic ones are:

- The team don't know the critical success factors for the project and, if they do, are they the same set as the management?

- Whining. People like to moan and this not a bad thing,... but it can be if no one listens.

- No names of real people involved appear on progress reports. This is a sign of lack of involvement with the project (or at least, lack of recognition and that is no better).

- A team thrown together and not selected for the right mix of skills and personality.

- The appearance of the new Jobsworth, a creature created by the environment, whereby if you succeed, you may be praised but if you fail, you will be chastised. So the logical thing is to not to risk anything. This is a management problem induced by the environment you make your people work in.

- Lack of an informal meeting place, the removal of the coffee point, the inference that people talking to each other are not working. After all, the manager has his coffee in his office—why should the troops have a break.

Looking outward from the team's point of view, there are a number of warning signs that apply, primarily, to the management of projects:

- The manager's closed door and/or lack of feedback.

- The overmanaged project, meetings bloody meetings, reports for reporting sake, people who feel they cannot do creative work due to the time spent on panic or ad hoc activities.

- The manager that throws people at the problem. Since the publication of the *Mythical Man Month* in 1975 we have all known that if you have a project that is running late and you throw more people at it, it will (most likely) become even more delayed. Despite this, it is still the most common response.

- Organisation charts with breaks, myriad dotted lines or simply no correspondence to reality.

- The accommodation police. Their aim is to get the maximum number of people into the smallest space. This is their key driver, irrespective of the effect on productivity, morale, etc.

- Too much tidiness. Is there a link between the clear desk and the empty mind?

- When management is replaced by schemes, attitude surveys, Incentive programmes and quality awards, etc.

- When activity is mistaken for productivity.

- Management by objectives which are linked to bonus. It is not unknown for these objectives to be met at the cost of cutting too many corners.

Some of the classic early warning signs from the customer's point of view are listed below—but first, an alternative definition of a customer.

The definition of a customer should be someone who has bought your services before and has come back for more. Until they return for the second time they can only really be considered a punter, not a customer.

It can be bad to lose a punter (although there are most certainly some punters you do not want in the first place). It is horrendous to lose a customer. How do you make sure it doesn't happen? Look for the early warning signs!

The worrying signs are:

- When the requirements are not provided by the real customer or end user and are not reviewed.

- The customer is not involved with the development of the project at all stages.

- The customer's perception is that the project does not aim to delight them and will argue about the contract on production of the product. This is a classic sign of failure. By not managing the customer's expectations, you will lose the customer. Perception is the key to future business.

- Are the NFRs (Non Functional Requirements) of the product prioritised and agreed with the customer?

Returning to the medical analogy, so far we have covered the work of the general practitioner; we now need to look at the specialist and ancillary workers and link these to the job of a software manager.

- The psychologists look at the people aspects. A healthy project must be based on committed people.

- The geriatricians will look after the old projects. Those that have delivered a useful product that needs to be kept in line with changing needs. The authors know of at least one software project now due for its silver jubilee.

- The undertakers will decently dispose of the dead project after the pathologists have found the cause of death and passed on the lessons learned. This should apply equally well to successfully completed as well as failed projects. There is evidence, though, that we are still making the same mistakes again and again.

- The curing of the sick project will be the function of the immunologists and, if they fail, the surgeons.

- The midwives who deliver the young project into live operation. The customer engineering role identified in Figure 3.4.

- The pathologists who study, analyse and improve the process. This is often a key role of senior management and relies for its effectiveness on good information (from process audits, customer feedback, etc).

Looking at each of the areas in turn, the physcologists will look at the people aspects by looking at communication and team building. The undertaker and geriatrician will look at the product with a view to minimise its costs as it nears the end of its useful life. This means they must know the state of each software project and hence their interest will be in configuration management, change control and product support.

The midwife will sort the interface between the stages of the project. The average woman has up to nine months warning to prepare for the birth. How long do average testers in a project get to familiarise themselves with the development before it lands on their desk to test? This is just one example of the interfaces in the project; there are many others and all are a possible risk, if not managed. The pathologists will concern themselves mainly with the process to try to determine the cause of any problems.

Managers of software projects have, at times, to take on all of these roles (which is why they usually go home shattered at the end of each day.) But what can be done about it? First take a lesson from National Health Service managers. In a crisis they are excellent—they have a system that they stick to. It is well defined, strictly adhered to and everyone involved knows exactly what their role is.

The other major thing to remember is that the production of software is a creative process and is usually done on the roll.

The function of the manager is to provide and maintain the environment to encourage and maintain the roll. Lots of enthusiasm and drive can sweep away surprising amounts of doubt and confusion.

4.7 WHERE TO LOOK

Over the life of a real project, problems occur. But where is the body of evidence that points you to the disaster-prone project? Most of this information is either old or based solely on projects from the USA. This may, or may not, be valid with the differences in methods of software engineering and the advances of technology.

We have analysed data from a number of projects using the problem reports and have produced the following results, by splitting the software project down into four main areas: requirements, design, installation and maintenance[1].

The object of this was to find where most faults were actually caused. We make no claim on the statistical validity, as the sample was not very large, but in the absence of other modern data it acts as an indicator (and seems to stack up against observed practice). The percentage of faults by area was:

Requirements	38%
Design	23%
Installation	7%
Maintenance	32%

The 23% of faults caused in design seems to fit quite well with the actual expenditure on design (approximately 20% of whole-lifecycle costs). This seems a reasonable finding.

The combined percentage of faults caused post-design is 40%—again, a reasonable finding as it reflects the not inconsiderable amount of tweaking required after delivery to meet the real customer requirements.

The problems in the requirements area are more worrying. They were typically split into two sub areas of functional and non-functional requirements. The majority of the problems were in the non-functional area, which relates to the quality aspects of the supplied system—performance, reliability, usability and the like.

This data may point to a communication problem between the customer and the supplier. Often, the product functioned but the customer's perception was that it was not what they wanted—usually the system did not perform as quickly as it needed to or was not well suited to the user's way of working.

---

[1] Maintenance is defined here as any changes made after acceptance by the customer.

Overall, the results support one of the main tenets of this chapter—that the main problem with software engineering is not technology but communication of the business need into a delivered product.

4.8 SUMMARY

This chapter has outlined some of the real symptoms of a sick project. Since different symptoms are observed by different people, the focus has been on defining a structured approach to finding the three or four small signs which, if spotted early on in a project, can save considerable surgery later on.

To summarise some of the key points in the chapter, here is a symptom checklist:

- Do you put people first, second, third and fourth? If you solve the people problems the technology will follow? You cannot solve people problems with technology.

- Do you preserve and protect successful teams? (The learning curve for new teams can be very long.)

- Do you know the success criteria for the project and is it the same for the team and for the management?

- Management should focus on providing strategic not tactical direction (give teams the right direction and the right tools and they will finish the job).

- The most efficient technology transfer is by moving in the people with the skills to seed the team.

- Some measures, any measure, will help. There is evidence that if you are seen to be measuring, your productivity will increase, the exception to this is when the measures are used to evaluate personal productivity or performance.

REFERENCES

[RN90] Rigby P and Norris M (1990) The software death cycle *Proc. UK IT 90 Conference (March, 1990)*

[Pre88] Pressman R S (1988) *Making Software Engineering Happen* Prentice-Hall

[NR92] Norris M and Rigby P (1992) *Software Engineering Explained* John Wiley & Sons

[DML] De Marco T and Lister T (1987) *Peopleware* Dorset House

[Pos87] Posner B Z (1987) What it takes to be a good project manager *Project Management* (March 1987)

[Pet85] Peters T (1985) *Thriving on Chaos, A Handbook for a Management Revolution* Pan Books

5

The Medicine Chest

A desperate disease requires a dangerous remedy

Guy Fawkes

If the alarm bells are triggered by the 'early warning system' outlined in the previous chapter—what should you do?

Recognition that there is a problem is a first step towards getting a project back on track. Recovery is not easy, though. It is a long-term process that must be planned strategically. It cannot be effected within a few weeks and requires continuous effort across those key areas identified at the beginning of the book. In this chapter, we will look in detail at what needs to be done with the People, to the Process and to the Product to bring the project back on track.

The first and, perhaps, the most important factor is the people. Sick projects are often great fun to work on and there is frequently significant reluctance to bring in the necessary control mechanisms to recover them. This resistance is not confined to those working at the 'sharp end' who thrive on firefighting, designing on the fly and on-site bug fixing. The project managers (and even the customers themselves) are sometimes content to work from the seat of the pants rather than to spend time planning, collecting statistics and devising future strategy. Getting 'buy-in' to a more controlled approach, and striking the balance between freedom of action and bureaucracy on the project, are not easy.

Once there is some commitment to change, the appropriate procedures and controls can be devised. There are a number of basic aspects of a software development project that need to be kept in order before it can be considered to be healthy. These range from the clear definition of project interfaces (e.g. making sure that local project plans make sense in the context of the customer's requirement) to the vital technical issues of configuration management, process measurement, etc. Once these basics are in place, an objective recovery plan can begin.

Finally, there is the product. The sick project is characterised by the fact that no-one has much idea of how the product will perform once released. It may prove reliable and satisfy all the user's needs, or it may require extensive rework before it is fit for purpose. As soon as the people start working to a defined process, early evaluation becomes possible and releasing a product of known quality becomes a possibility.

5.1   HOW DO YOU WIN OVER THE PEOPLE?

Change is rarely popular, even when a need for change is apparent.

There are good and bad ways of managing change and the prime differentiator is the way in which the plans for change are communicated. A number of actions and guidelines are outlined below. These need to be actively managed as part of any recovery programme [Sto90]. If they are not given due care and attention, all the tools, techniques and procedures described later on are unlikely to yield benefit.

Some of the essential actions in the recovery stage are as follows.

Explain the need for change

As stated earlier, sick projects can be great fun. They can seem to be going well when viewed from within, so it is important to put the need for change into context. It should be seen not as a blame exercise, more as a course correction. If it is clear that targets are not being met, for whatever reason, then a new approach is required. There are several options for this 'new approach'. These include the cancellation of the project, the imposition of a new way of working and the building of a consensus plan for recovery. The first two are sometimes the right way to go—cancellation is appropriate if the project is not just sick but dead, and the imposition of a recovery plan may work if one individual is prepared to take the entire burden. In most cases it is the consensus route that works. There is little advice that can be given for the first two cases so the guidelines below assume that consensus is the chosen option.

Outline the plans, take feedback and then take decisions.

A recovery plan needs to be evolved. It should start with the overall project aims (e.g. the objectives of the project stakeholders, the criteria for success, the vision of what is to be achieved, etc) and should be built in conjunction with all those who have to realise the overall aims. The total quality management approach to problem solving applies very well to this exercise. Some of the relevant TQM techniques are covered in Appendix 3.

Review progress against plans

When the criteria for project success are defined, some of the milestones towards achieving them need to be defined [You90]. Specific objectives help gauge progress. The setting of objectives is also useful for individuals but it is important here to give space for achievement. Impossible goals are, at best, achieved; stretching ones may be exceeded.

Explain decisions

It is not practical to operate by consensus for any more than a short period. It is vital therefore that project decisions taken in day-to-day running are explained properly. Sensible decisions can seem anything but, unless the thinking behind them is exposed.

Define roles, delegate tasks

If change is to be succesful, everyone needs to play a part and everyone has to understand the part they play (e.g. release manager, design authority, customer liaison). Simple job descriptions go a long way to ensuring that people know what they are expected to contribute [DML87].

To complement the above actions, there are ten guidelines for achieving a successful project.

1 A sense of purpose

It must be clear to all concerned why the project is going on at all. If people cannot see what they are working towards, they will not be well placed to contribute their best. It is not enough to have an abstract goal: the sense of purpose must be relevant to what people actually do. The London Metropolitan Police found this out when they tried to set objectives for the force. It was soon clear that the objectives were having little impact. No-one understood them until they were related to day-to-day, local issues.

2 Small teams

Groups of about five or six people are usually the most effective teams. The converse is often true—large teams, ten or more, are less effective. This does not mean that there is an inherent maximum project size. Rather that the project needs to be broken down into well defined tasks that can be tackled with a small team.

3 Owned processes

Software projects are usually complex and there is a need for common procedures. These should not all be imposed on those managing the project. The most effective procedures are those devised by the people carrying out the work. This is partly because they match reality, partly because the people who have to use the procedure are committed to it.

4 Balanced teams

Great teams are rarely comprised of all innovators, all visionaries or all implementors. Different people do different things well and, although free choice is often not an option, some attention should be paid to the balance of skills within a team. The authors have observed time and again that teams of brilliant individuals often disappoint while less gifted teams with a balance of personalities succeed. The work of, for instance, Belbin [Bel82] provides some of the necessary tools for achieving a good team balance.

5 Balance of skills

Just as people's personalities differ, so do their areas of expertise. A good user-interface designer may not be a good database designer and vice versa. Small teams work by concentrating expertise on a well defined target, so it is important to ensure that the target and the team skills are well matched.

6 Plan the overview, not the detail

Many projects get lost in a welter of detail—plans showing every single activity and dependancy, system designs that show every item of data and process. Too much detail becomes unmanageable in the face of inevitable change. On the other hand it is vital to establish the half dozen or so, core processes upon which the project is founded. The overall picture of even the biggest project should become clear by looking at these core processes.

7 Encourage error detection

People are often castigated for making mistakes and see their errors being revealed as a threat. This has some virtue in encouraging attention to detail but does give rise to a major problem, especially in software projects. Errors that could be eradicated at the early stages of a project are carried forward into later stages. Since the cost of fixing an error rises by a factor of ten for every stage of the project [Boe81] it makes a lot of sense to motivate people to find bugs early. It is not enough simply to introduce techniques such as those in the previous section—early eradication of errors must be a prime project goal. This idea can be extended by preventing a project from moving between stages (e.g. specification and design) until there are no detectable defects—a zero defect methodology—with well defined entry and exit conditions to each stage in the process.

8 Keep technical people, technical

The traditional way to reward a good technical person is to make them a manager. This is a very hit and miss approach as it depletes technical resources on the promise of developing management resource. The recognition of technical and management contributions needs to be on a par—a chief architect is as vital to project success as a project manager!

9 Keep timescales short

Early and regular victories are the lifeblood of a successful project. If no external progress is visible from a project for nine months or more, then there is cause for concern. Any project should aim to have something relevant to demonstrate every few months, at least. This not only maintains a feeling of progress within the project, it also helps to manage customer expectations (and minimise step changes in requirements).

10 Support the project

All projects are different and they all have their own technical and organisational characteristics. A small amount of time and effort should be invested in providing the few, key enabling tools (e.g. a problem-reporting log, a task scheduler, a data cross referencer, etc) that enable the team to function efficiently.

The key message of this section is that it is vital to have a team committed to a healthy project. The simple fact is that managing the people side of recovery is not easy—and there are few hard and fast rules to help. The actions and guidelines above are a useful start but active management is essential for success. The sections below are comparitively rich in specific techniques but should not divert attention from the fact that recovery is what people are motivated to make of it.

5.2   HOW DO YOU CLASSIFY THE PROCESS?

In essence, a process is no more than a collection of procedures that together define how the job gets done. There are many ways of evaluating how 'good' a process is (often referred to as the level of process maturity) and of ensuring that you measure the vital few parameters that will give a basis for improving it.

The base levels of process maturity are now well established in terms of quality management [NR92]. Before going on to look at specific process maturity models, it is worth briefly reviewing the stages of process maturity. These can be summarized as:

- *Anarchy*. No systematic control of any part of the process—there is freedom to do whatever is expedient.

- *Stability (quality assurance)*. This brings some order out of chaos and provides a core process for software development. In some cases there is no justification other than the belief that 'it will feel better'[1].

- *Measurement and control (quality control)*. For software, measurement can only be achieved in a stable environment where the process (at least) is identifiable and repeatable. Measurement of process and product is required to enable real control.

- *Improve (quality improvement)*. No real world process is perfect, so improvements, based on observation of current practice, are always possible.

- *Theory (quality by design)*. Once a process is well understood, underlying theories that explain cause and effect can be developed.

Most software projects specify at least some procedures to define the various operations in product development; for instance, the format and naming conventions for documentation, coding standards, review procedures, etc. This introduces some basic stability into the software development process. The general idea of defining the process is to:

- Write down what you are doing.

- Do it.

- Prove that you are doing it.

---

[1] This contrasts with manufacturing industries, where measurement precedes stability. The non-repetitive nature of software projects has, historically, made it easier to control the process as the first step.

This is the approach that underpins all of the current software quality assurance registration standards such as BS5750, ISO9000 and AQAP [RSN89]. Recovery will only work once this level of control over development is installed. It then becomes possible to record statistics and to determine some basis for overall improvement (e.g. by identifying common problem areas).

There are, however, no guarantees that control over the process really helps with either the people or the product. Specifically, a set of procedures which guide the operation of the organisation put few constraints on what is actually produced. They simply provide a framework for its production. Also, from the people point of view, procedures that specify 'how' to do a task, but not 'why', can appear irrelevant. In this instance, there is little chance of any commitment to them.

An improvement programme relies on amending a process based on observation and measurement of how it currently performs. This means assessing a process in terms of how people *actually* use it and how good the final product *really* is.

An effective and relatively straightforward means of doing this is to carry out a software process 'Healthcheck'. The idea here is to establish a gross picture of which aspects of the process are working well and which are not by asking the people on the project a standard set of questions. For a medium sized project team (up to 40) this usually takes no more than a day for one or two people. An example standard set of questions (covering all the major development activities such as design, testing, project management, maintenance) is reproduced in Appendix 1.

Once complete, the results of the 'healthcheck' can be presented as in Figure 5.1. This shows the *perceived* process effectiveness in each area against best known practice. The ideal would be to have all ratings at the end of the radial axes.

Although far from rigorous, the 'healthcheck' does highlight the major areas of concern. Also, it is simple to install as an ongoing measure of the local process and is easy to support with simple tools (e.g. Figure 5.2 shows the format of the authors' 'healthcheck advisor'). This type of process check complements the project quality audits that would be carried out as part of ISO9001 [NR92]. Together they give a good indication of the technical and procedural status of the project—a firm base for improvement.

A more sophisticated (and hence more expensive) way of assessing a process is to compare it against a common standard, the best known of which is the Software Engineering Institute's Capability Maturity Model [SEI91]. This defines five levels of process maturity (from Level 1-initial, through Level 2-repeatable, to Level 4-Managed and Level 5-optimised). As with the 'healthcheck', the SEI assessment is derived from a series of questions (over 120 of them) set in terms of project activities that should be carried, standards that should be in place and abilities that should be evident.

Assessment against the SEI model is considerably more objective (and so takes longer) than the Healthcheck described above. For instance a

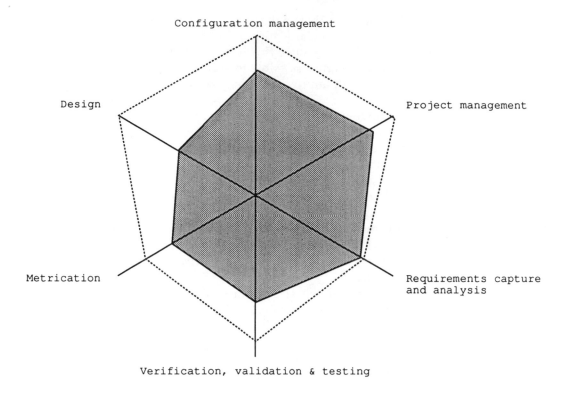

Figure 5.1   The software 'healthcheck'

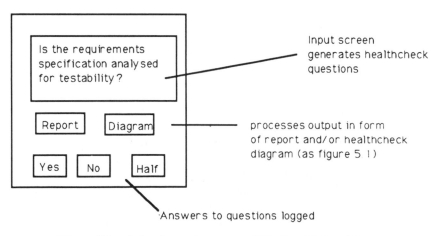

Figure 5.2   A simple tool to support the 'healthcheck'

medium sized project would take two people around 2–3 weeks to assess. Once complete, though, the results give a tranferable rating of process maturity within the framework shown in Figure 5.3

Process standards are likely to become increasingly adopted over the next few years. The SEI model is already well established in the USA and an internationally recognised (ISO-SPICE) version is planned for 1995. The contents of this international standard are likely to be built on the SEI model and the areas covered are likely to be similar; for instance, at Level 2, in the process is Software Project Planning, for which the *activities* include:

- that actual expenditure over time and work completed are compared with plan (activity 5)

- that technical, cost resource and schedule risks are tracked through the project (activity 9)

- that actual measured data and replanning data are recorded for later use (activity 10)

Level	Characteristic	Key Problem Area
5 – Optimizing Emphasis on defect prevention	Improvement fed back into process	Automation
4 – Managed Measurable basis for process improvement	Measured process (quantitative)	Problem analysis Problem prevention Technology management
3 – Defined Standard process is defined for all projects	Process defined	Process measurement Process analysis Qualitative quality plans
2 – Repeatable Similar projects done in the same way	Process depends on individuals	Training Reviews and Testing Standards
1 – Initial Every project handled differently	Ad hoc process	Project Management Project planning Configuration management

Figure 5.3 The SEI maturity model

and the *abilities* include:

● that software managers receive training in estimating and tracking software costs and schedules.

In order to advance to Level 3, an organisation must have moved from this level of control to having a software process that is stable and under statistical process control. The abilities at this level require training in the selection, collection and validation of process measurement data and the application of statistical methods.

It is worth pointing out that the process assessment techniques described here are strongly related. Since they all rely on scoring against a set of predetermined questions, they can be presented in a common format, as shown in Figure 5.4. This is useful when the process assessment has to be to a common standard (e.g. SEI-CMM) but also requires (usually for local purposes) a finer granularity than the standard allows.

A more detailed explanation of process measures is given in Appendix 1.

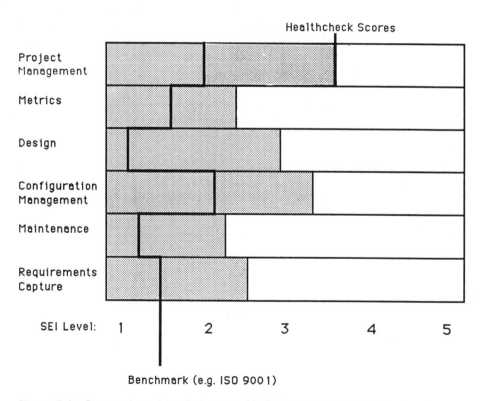

Figure 5.4   Process benchmark showing SEI-CMM and healthcheck scores

5.3 HOW DO YOU MEASURE THE PRODUCT?

It is often the case that the first sign of a poor quality product comes when it fails under test. This is better than it falling over the first time the customer comes to use it but is far from ideal. There are many points through the software development process at which an objective assessment of the product characteristics can be made [KNP93]. It is quite feasible to draw up an 'assessment lifecycle' for software products and Figure 5.5 shows where the key assessment points can be placed.

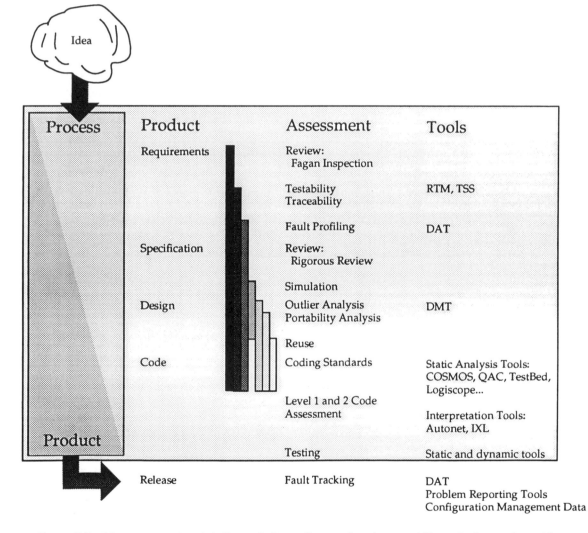

Figure 5.5 Measurement points through the software development lifecycle (reproduced by permission of British Telecommunications plc)

There is, inevitably, a cost associated with each product assessment carried out. In many cases this is small: a question of good practice rather than expensive tools or training. Some assessment techniques do require investment to install but can provide considerable benefit.

A brief description for each of the procedures and techniques shown in Figure 5.5 is given below. Each one is included here on the basis that it has been shown in practice to provide considerable cost/benefit advantage. The last part of this section summarizes the costs, the payback and specific areas of application of these assessment methods.

Requirements

At this early stage in the lifecycle, the key question to be addressed is whether it will be possible to check that the stated requirements are satisfied by the final implementation. The extent to which each requirement can be satisfied by a defined test case [Bei86] provides a reasonable measure of its practicality. Figure 5.6 shows a typical requirements test matrix used to provide this measure.

This is a very simple practice to adopt yet provides considerable benefit: statements like 'it will be easy to learn' and 'messages will be delivered in real time' can be recast, respectively, as 'an average user should be able to logon to and exit from the application within one hour' and 'average network transit delay should not exceed 50ms under average loading'.

In addition to helping clarify requirements, this technique provides the starting place for generating the acceptance tests for the finished product.

4 Reqs validation matrix

Feature Reference		Description	Specification Reference	Test Case 1	2	3	4	5	6	7	8	9
Screens	0	LC/NC Start Case	Mobius	*	*	*			*			
Screens	1	LC-Data entry	Directive 0001	*	*	*			*	*		
Screens	2	LC-initial coordination	Directive 0030		*	*			*			
Screens	3	LC-Record local evaluation	Directive 0120			*	*					
Screens	4	LC-Estimate cost/benefit	Directive 0160						*			
Screens	5	LC-Review update	Directive 0230					*	*			
Screens	6	LC-Record IPU	Directive 0250						*			*
Screens	7	NC-National coordination	Directive 0125				*		*			*
Screens	8	NC-Estimate cost/benefit	Directive 0300					*	*			*
Screens	9	LC-Action national decision	Directive 0320							*	*	*
Screens	10	NC-QC review update	Directive 0330					*		*		
Screens	11	NC-Final savings update	Directive 0310							*		

Figure 5.6 A check for testability of requirements (reproduced by permission of British Telecommunication plc)

Specification

By the time that the specification for the product has been written, it is possible to provide some formal assessment of its soundness. This is usually done using one of the many walkthrough or review procedures [Hol91] that have proved to be very cost effective and are in routine use within many organisations. All walkthough and review techniques rely on the close scrutiny of a specification by a number of people. This flushes out many potential problems and often provides a better basis for implementation.

In some cases (e.g. safety or security critical applications) it is desirable to go one step further than peer review and prove the specification. Figure 5.7 outlines a technique, known as the rigorous review technique [ABS93], that can be used to detect those subtle errors that are often missed. This technique works by translating elements of a structured specification into a mathematically formal language, such as Z. During both the translation and subsequent analysis of the formal text, inconsistencies and omissions in the specification are revealed.

Design

A great number of tools have emerged over the last five years or so to help the software designer. Many of them ensure consistency and conformance to standards (i.e. that syntax is correct and method rules are followed). Some can automatically highlight potential problems within a design. Figure 5.8 shows the output from a design metrics tool that tries to encapsulate some of the 'rules of good design' in order to identify areas outside the norm.

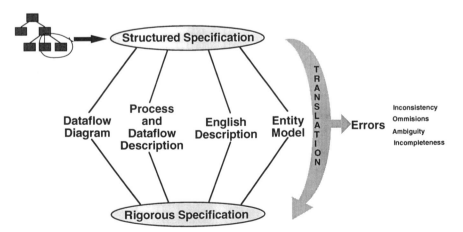

Figure 5.7   The rigorous review technique (reproduced by permission of British Telecommunications plc)

The Design Metrics Collection and Analysis Process

The cyclic diagram shown documents the process that is involved during design metrics collection and analysis.

The designer will create their design on a CASE tool, which in this case is the Software Through Pictures Tool. When the design is complete, the extraction tool STPtoDMT is run. It examines the contents of the STPdata dictionary, and creates a text file for each DFD, STD, ERD and SC designed using the tool.

These text files are then loaded into the Design Metrics Tool (DMT) which calculates various metrics. The DMT calculates 9 DFD and SC metrics, 4 ERD metrics and 5 STD metrics.

The metric values can be displayed in two forms; scatter plots and histograms. Designer and managers can examine these diagrams to spot any potential problem areas in the design by using the technique known as outlier analysis.

Outliers are data items that do not follow the trend or relationship that the majority of the data items are showing.

The metric values can be used as an input to a statistical package such as Minitab. It is a comprehensive statistical package which can be used to determine any underlying relationships between the metrics and the metric values.

The results of outlier analysis and statistical examination may uncover problems or potential problems with the design. The appropriate changes can then be made to the design.

As well as determining potential troublesome areas of the design, the metrics values may be used in any cost estimation process.

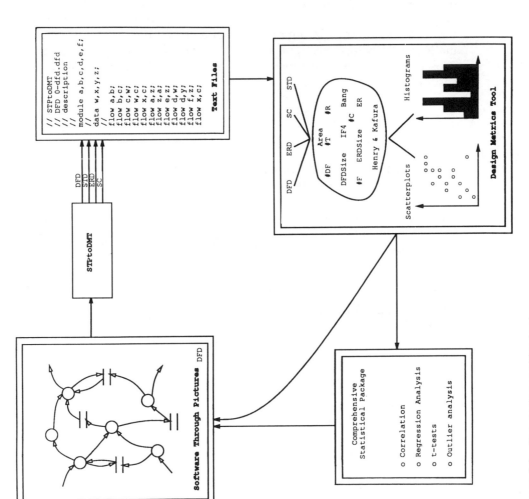

Figure 5.8 The design metrics tool

The use of such tools provides real-time feedback on the likely maintainability and reliability of a designer's output. This form of support ensures that good design practice is embedded in the development process, rather than being the preserve of key individuals.

Code

Code assessment, in the context of this book, is concerned with its likely reliability and maintainability rather than whether it operates as expected. There are two levels at which code assessment can be conducted:

- Level 1. This is a set of straightforward measures on the code—complexity of modules, information flows, etc. This level can be carried out using commercially available tools. Perhaps the most important aspect of this level is ensuring that the right measures are made. Figure 5.9, based on a number of observation studies, summarises the the most appropriate measures for a specific range of tasks to be accomplished (see also Appendix 2).

- Level 2. Even if the most appropriate measures are taken, they still have to be accurately interpreted. This is no easy matter: the observation studies described in [KNP93] require a considerable amount of skill to correctly identify the relationships between what was measured and how this is related to characteristics of the software. Once established, these relationships can be embedded in an expert system. This provides a reproducible means of carrying out code assessments.

Figure 5.10 shows how level 1 and level 2 fit together to provide a complete code evaluation scheme. This arrangement allows out of specification modules (which would likely prove problemmatical in the field) to be identified and, if required, reworked.

Test

The testing of software is, in itself, an assessment of the product. The completeness with which tests on software have been carried out is already well documented [Bei86].

Maintenance

One of the laws of software projects is that maintenance matters [NR92]—there is life after development. Since software systems spend most of their lives being maintained, post release, it makes sense to assess this phase with as much vigour as the development phases.

Metric family >	Size metrics			Control flow metrics											Inf flow
Recommended metrics > / Reason for collecting metrics	KLN	KLV(DO)	KLC(CO)	DEPDE	DEPWM	DEPSU	VINDE	VINSU	NUMWM	PRASU	BRTWM	SIMSU	MCCDE		HK
Quality:															
Predicting quality before testing															
1. Module correctness		▓		▓			▓	▓	▓	▓			▓		▓
2. Module fault density															
Predicting future quality at release															
1. Module correctness		▓		▓	▓	▓		▓	▓	▓	▓		▓		▓
2. Module fault density															
3. Module performance															
4. Module maintainability		▓													▓
5. Module code maintainability		▓													
Cost:															
Predicting costs at release															
1. Module maintainability		▓		▓	▓										▓
2. Module code maintainability		▓	▓	▓											

KLN = 000s of lines of non-comment source code
KLV = 000s of lines of variable declaration
KLC = 000s of lines of comment code
DEPDE = maximum depth of nesting, density version
DEPWM = maximum depth of nesting, weighted mean version
DEPSU = maximum depth of nesting, sum version
VINDE = the 'Product VINAP' metric, density version

VINSU = the 'Product VINAP' metric, sum version
NUMWM = the 'Number of Paths' metrics, weighted mean version
PRASU = the 'Prather' metric, sum version
BRTWM = the 'Branch Testing' metric, weighted mean version
SIMSU = the 'Number of Simple Paths' metric, sum version
MCCDE = the 'McCabe Cyclomatic Complexity' metric, density version
HK = Henry Kafura, an information flow measure

(DO) indicates a measure of data orientation
(CO) indicates a measure of communicativeness

Figure 5.9 Table of measures (reproduced by permission of British Telecommunications plc)

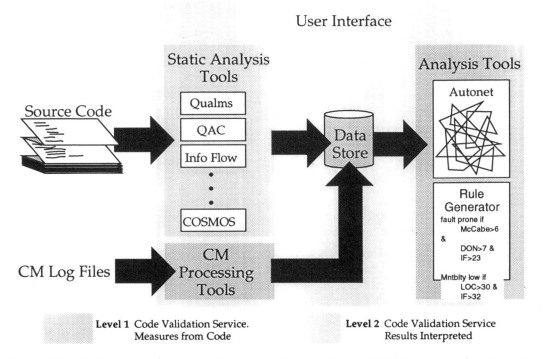

Figure 5.10   Tools for code assessment (reproduced by permission of British Telecommunications plc)

A simple but effective means of measuring how a product performs in maintenance is to collect and analyse reported faults. This can be easily automated—the output from a simple data analysis tool is shown in Figure 5.11a. This sort of tool can be used to provide reliability data on a product by recording the frequency with which faults are located as well as the place where the faults were found and the stage at which they were discovered.

There are a number of useful variants on Figure 5.11a that can provide insight into the effectiveness of maintenance. For instance, graphs showing the status of faults (raised, evaluated, implemented, cleared, etc) can be used to identify repair bottlenecks, etc.

Useful information for subsequent development projects can also be built up by identifying where released faults are first introduced—Figure 5.11b shows the stage at which problems were introduced into the product against the stage at which they were detected.

This type of assessment shows how effective the verification and validation techniques used during the early stages of the lifecycle actually are.

All of the techniques described in this section have been shown to be useful in assessing real software products. Deciding which of them to use is very much a matter of judgement and is strongly linked to your level of process maturity: the rigorous review technique described above would be useful to

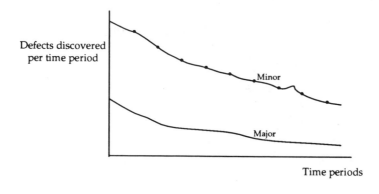

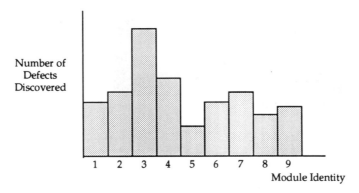

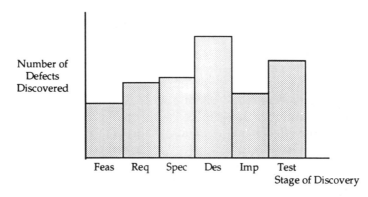

Figure 5.11a   Number of outstanding faults over time (reproduced by permission of British Telecommunications plc)

a Level 5 organisation but would not tackle the key problems of a Level 1 organisation (e.g. project stage reviews).

There are two useful pieces of information to help in choosing the appropriate techniques. The first is Figure 5.12a. This summarizes the relevant assessment techiques against each level of process maturity.

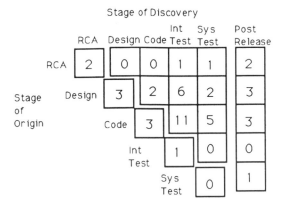

Figure 5.11b   Analysis of reported problems by stage of origin and detection (reproduced by permission of British Telecommunications plc)

Relevant techniques for
assessing the product

Level of Process Maturity		Relevant techniques for assessing the product
	1	– basic defect measurement – simple healthcheck – design reviews
	2	– regular healthcheck – routine defect measurement – formal review of requirements, design, code
	3	– defect analysis (root cause etc) – requirements testability – objective limits for requirements, design, code
	4	– rigorous design review – code assessed for likely maintainability
	5	– automated product assessment – predictions of quality based on previous project data

Figure 5.12a   Assessment techniques by level of process maturity

The second is Figure 12b which shows the typical root causes of system errors—where the product goes wrong in the first place. These two, together with cost/benefit analysis allow a realistic assessment plan covering the whole product development to be drawn up.

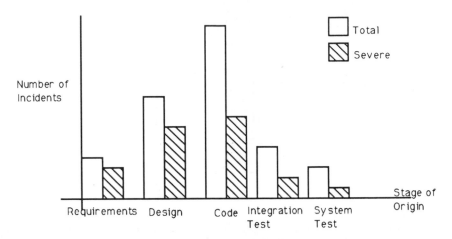

Figure 5.12b   Root causes of system errors (reproduced by permission of British Telecommunications plc)

One final guideline is to examine exactly what measures are required—in the words of M J Moroney, 'Data should be collected with a clear purpose in mind. Not only a clear purpose, but clear idea as to the precise way in which they will be analysed so as to yield the desired information.'

The product assessment lifecycle and techniques described above provide a valuable counterpoint to the more traditional approach of measuring the development process against a quality schedule, such as ISO9001. Together they allow the thorough examination of a software project and, once the people who work on the projects are committed to recovery, enable improving health to be measured.

A more detailed explanation of product measures is given in Appendix 2. This covers the definition of measures (e.g. code complexity, information flow) along with how they can be extracted and interpreted. The next chapter moves on from what is available to stimulate and measure recovery to its practical application.

5.4   SUMMARY

Once a sick project has been identified, a plan of action to recover it can be put in place. There are no simple or quick remedies for this but there are a number of effective guidelines that will, if diligently pursued, lead to recovery. This chapter has outlined how the people, process and product factors can be tackled, from simple but vital team building through to specific techniques such as specification auditing.

Project recovery is far from being an exact science, though. To be successful it first requires all members of the project team to buy in to a common vision of what is to be achieved. It must then be planned in terms of technical activities, quality procedures and team organisation. Finally it must be treated as a long term project in its own right—the recovery of a large project can often take one to two years to be fully effective.

Earlier in this chapter ten golden rules for successful projects were suggested. The process and product measurement techiques given towards the end of the chapter can be used to turn these golden rules into practice:

1. Foster a common sense of purpose within the project.
2. Keep the separate project teams small.
3. Ensure that processes are owned by the people that use them.
4. Balance the types of people within the teams.
5. Recognise the need for a range of different skills.
6. Plan and maintain the overview, not the detail.
7. Encourage error detection at all stages.
8. Keep technical people, technical.
9. Keep timescales short and victories regular.
10. Support the project by resourcing its infrastructure.

These provide a useful checklist for assessing how far down the road to recovery you are and, when compared against some of the pitfalls mentioned in Chapter 4, help to ensure that it is not the empty milestones that make the most noise.

REFERENCES

[ABS93] Aujla S, Bryant A and Semmens L (1993) Rigorous review technique *Proc Software Engineering Standards Conf (Brighton, 1993)*

[Bei86] Beizer B (1983) *Software Testing Techniques* Van Nostrand Rheinhold

[Bel82] Belbin M (1982) *Effective Teams*

[Boe81] Boehm W B (1981) *Software Engineering Economics* Prentice-Hall

[DML87] DeMarco T and Lister T (1987) *Peopleware* Dorset House

[Hol91] Hollicker C (1991) *Software Review and Audit Handbook* John Wiley & Sons

[KNP93] Karkaria D, Norris M and Pengelly A (1993) Software product assessment *BT Technology Journal* vol11 no1

[NR92] Norris M and Rigby P (1992) *Software Engineering Explained* John Wiley & Sons

[RSN89] Rigby P, Stoddart A and Norris M 1989 Assuring quality in software—practical experience of attaining ISO9001 *BT Engineering Journal* vol 8 no 4

[SEI91] Software Engineering Institute, Carnegie-Mellon University 1991 *Software Capability Maturity Model*

[Sto90] Stockman S G (1990) The recovery of software projects *Proc. 1st European Software QA Conference , (Brussels 1990)*

[You90] Youll D (1990) *Making Software Development Visible—Effective Project Control* John Wiley & Sons

6

Kill or Cure

Laws too gentle are seldom obeyed, too severe, seldom executed

Benjamin Franklin

In the previous chapter we outlined the symptoms of a sick project and proposed some measures, postulated who should do the measurement and why they should do it. This chapter is about what to do once you *know* how sick the project is.

This can be gauged from the early warning signs and measures proposed in Chapter 5. But, as already stated, beware of the holy grail of metrication, the single metric. Any one measure is of little value unless it is linked to others and you need a cross section of useful and relevant measures before the true picture emerges. A useful image is that of the car dashboard with a set of instruments. Here, a reading of zero on the oil pressure guage is no problem when the engine is stopped but may give cause for concern when doing 80 mph on the motorway! The use of more than one measure is essential to avoid concentration on one area to the detriment of others. This chapter will, for simplicity, be split up into the three Ps but when considering recovery all three areas must be considered simultaneously.

We are now in a position to plan recovery of the project but remember the medical statement 'the operation was a success but the patient died.'

The key is business survival and to accomplish this you may have to kill projects. This may seem heresy to some people—power or success is sometimes equated with number of people or size of budget. But if these do not contribute to success, they are false gods. As with people, it is the quality of life of software that is important not mere survival. An invalid software project can cost a fortune to keep.

In this chapter we will outline the factors to be taken into account and propose some recovery routes. The major metric in any decision will be money—

this is the key driver for all kill or cure decisions. Money is a single metric, admittedly, but all other metrics can be considered sub-metrics of it.

6.1   EUTHENASIA OR RECOVERY?

The decision must be based on the business case (assuming there is one) for the project. The business case should have outlined the reasons for doing this project—to make money, to give a strategic advantage (and hence make money), to improve safety (and save money) etc. The project plans will have to be assessed in the light of the current position of the project and the likely cost of recovery.

Then it is crunch time—to kill or not to kill?

But first a few pointers. A software project is essentially a cognitive exercise and the team involved may love their baby. No matter how bad the project there will always be someone to defend it. Typical statements are 'We have spent X thousand pounds on this project. If we just spend another few pounds we will get it back on course' and 'This software is the core of the future projects.' We all know what happens to an apple whose core is rotten!

Another problem is that a bad project usually means lots of firefighting, which can be fun to all who have been involved (for a short while). It brings out the Rambo in managers and allows the most introverted member of the team to be noisy and rush about, eventually reaching the stage where all activity can be confused with productivity.

But don't be fooled. Most of the team will know the real health of the project and would prefer to produce quality products in a stable environment (and see more of their families).

The consequence of these factors is that, once a decision has been made to terminate a project, it must be communicated quickly to the team involved as well as senior management or the customer. There is nothing more demoralising, and hence team destroying, than working on a dead project—especially if you haven't been told that it is dead.

The killing of a project can be seen as personal failure by the project manager (and it often is) but these feelings must be tempered with sound financial information. Never forget that software maintenance (the cost of future ownership) accounts for, on average, between 50% and 70% of the whole-lifecycle cost of software. An invalid will cost even more. Better short-term pain for long-term gain.

The object at this stage is to define the risk of keeping or stopping the project. One technique to help you to decide the course of action is Cost Benefit Analysis which is a technique for comparing the cost of taking a particular set of actions with the benefits achievable from their outcome. It is a method of assessing the viability of the courses of action in monetary terms. The key steps are:

- Determine the period of the analysis. (How long will it be before return on investment is required?)

- Determine the factors (people's time, equipment, company reputation, market alternatives, technical options, etc).

- Value the factors (e.g. cost of development, cost of failure, cost of buying externally, etc).

- Analyse and evaluate the information.

The period of analysis is for you to decide but the predicted life of the software product may be a good start. But you must be realistic. If the cost of recovery is more than the profit, the action is clear—kill the project now! If not, below are some recovery methods which only you can model.

6.2 RECOVERY

The decision has now been made that the project must recover and in doing so will benefit the financial health of the company. This process should start with risk analysis; if not, detailed planning is to little effect and there is a real danger of grabbing defeat from the jaws of victory. The biggest gains, but hardest to achieve at this stage and in fact all subsequent stages, will be by involving the team. This is the first of the three Ps to be tackled

The medical analogy can still be applied to the the recovery of software projects here. Convalescence can be a long process needing careful nursing (management) and the right environment and treatment (again the responsibility of management). The project may, like a patient, also be subject to relapses and, sometimes, unexpected complications. But by this stage you should have done the cost benefit analysis. Hence the commitment to success should be high (otherwise, the recovery would not have been attempted). If it is not, then further action is required by the management of the project.

From the above you will see the recovery of a project is almost totally dependent upon skilful and sensitive management and team leadership. The recovery is a game of inches putting right the most pressing problems first.

In Chapter 4 we showed that one of the major reasons for project failure is poor communications. We know all managers are good communicators—they would not have the job if they were not. But communication must be Duplex not Simplex. In other words, it is not enough to tell the team what to do. Listening is also key. For instance, there is considerable value in presenting the cost benefit and risk analysis and taking comments from the team on them. This often reveals something about the project you did not know and will, in effect, relaunch the project and get you to the first base in getting buy-in to the recovery process.

The next step is to look at the team. Is it fit for the recovery task and do you have the right mix? There are many learned tomes on team selection for success but to be frank, at this stage you won't have the time to read them. There are a few rules of thumb.

- Adding extra staff to a late project may make it even later (throwing people at the problem is not the answer).

- Move the Jonahs (the person who refuses to believe that there may be some light at the end of the tunnel) out of the team. It is better to lose their experience than infect the rest of the team (and watch for the new Jobsworth).

- Look for and encourage signs of a healthy organisation. The signs are that it:

  - Makes a cult of Quality.

  - Provides lots of satisfactory closes.

  - Builds a sense of eliteness.

  - Allows and encourages hetrogeneity.

  - Works on strategic not tactical direction.

We now know the state of the people involved in the project. If the recovery is to be sustained you need quick victories so the rule is little and often and publish the successes. Goals that can be achieved in short timescales are a great confidence and team builder. These goals have to be planned, achieved and celebrated to keep the momentum of recovery going.

6.3   THE TECHNICAL OPTIONS

One of the problems with a sick project is that even if the trouble is not terminal, some action will almost always be required. The previous chapters have given you the symtoms and available medicine—you now need to decide on the remedial action to take. This may be technical or organisational, or both.

The technical options open to a project manager are dependent on how ill the project is. Some of the options are:

1. Complete re-analysis of the requirements before redevelopment.
2. Programme rewrites.
3. Code analysis and restructuring.
4. Code analysis and redesign.
5. Improve change control procedures.
6. Improve documentation.
7. Do nothing.

The above list in desending order of severity needs to be expanded to encompass benefits, disadvantages and cost. The object is to allow for some risk analysis information to enable the decision on which action to take.

Complete re-analysis of requirements before full redevelopment

Description

- This is, in fact, replacement of the system. Any earlier work can be considered as an expensive requirements capture exercise. Redevelopment is by far the most radical and costly cure for a sick project and will be motivated by the diagnosis producing the worst symptoms of project failure. These will include the existing system not meeting the customer's need and changes to the system which no longer reflect an extension of the original purpose of the system. The manifestations of this problem may be in the form of major changes in architecture or technology to try to rapidly fix the problem or by a constant stream of change requests as the customer or pseudo customer realise the product will not do.

Benefits

- New system will meet most of the customer's requirements.
- Future change requests are not likely to be so drastic or as numerous.
- The customer should now fully understand their requirements.

Disadvantages

- An open admission of failure by the project team.
- System requirement will have to be redone.
- The project will have to be totally replanned and rescheduled.
- The development costs, resources and timescales will increase.
- The amount of reuse of parts of the old project may be limited due to a loss of faith by the project staff.

Costs

- Large or very large as the project will have to cover the whole lifecycle cost of the new project from requirements capture to test and maintenance. If you can keep the existing team the learning curve should be relatively short.

Programme rewrites

Description

- Rewrites are performed at the programme or module level. The motivation for a rewrite is most likely to be to provided by the difficulties in testing a particularly complex area of code. It may be a module that is particularly bug ridden or requires a disproportionate amount of analysis effort when undergoing changes, due to lack of adequate standards.

Benefits

- Programs can be rewritten selectively.
- Programs can be rewritten as resources allow.
- Allows the production of good test cases for the key areas of the program or key modules.
- Greater user and customer satisfaction.

Disadvantages

- Assumes system design is sound.
- Time and resource consuming.
- Extensive testing required.

Costs

- There will be a need for extra staff for testing but this will be less than for a full redesign.

Code analysis and restructuring

Description

- Depending on the language there are tools and services available for the automatic and semi-automatic analysis of code. These tools will report on:

  - The complexity of existing structure.
  - Parts of the code that are unreachable.
  - Which programs that will most benefit from restructuring.

Benefits

- Lower-cost alternative to rewriting or redevelopment.

- Faults will be easier to find.

- Logic faults may be easier to unravel.

- Short timescale, low level of disruption to the users.

- Useful when system works and no redesign is required.

- Useful when redesign is required but urgent action is needed now.

Disadvantages

- Assumes no change in the user requirements.

- System testing will still be required to verify that original functionality has been preserved in the restructured system.

- No automatic correction of errors.

- Skilled manual intervention will be required with some programme logic.

Costs

- The purchase and training for the use of a tool and the employment of extra staff.

Code analysis and redesign

Description

- In this case the physical implementation is replaced without regard to re-examining the existing logical system. There is no requirements phase except to ensure that the existing system specification is complete before redesign is commenced. The difference between system redesign and program rewrites is the level of system abstraction at which the work is done. Program rewrites will almost certainly include an amount of redesign but at a low level.

Benefits

- No costly requirements capture phase required.

- New system will conform to new site standards.

- Test cases will be properly documented.
- Removal of errors in the system.
- Can improve the data handling system.

Disadvantages

- Assumes no change in user's requirements.
- Additional resources are required.
- Cannot be introduced piecemeal.

Costs

- This will involve a study and an investment appraisal.

Improve change control procedures with the old system

Description

- If the change control procedures are found to be lacking or deficient, then establishment and enforcement of them is a priority; this also applies to documentation.

Benefit

- Reduction of loosely written, badly structured code—the changes are reviewed and monitored and therefore the coding can be supervised.
- Life expectancy of the system will increase.
- Maintenance will be easier and transferable to third parties if required.
- Should stop the uncontrolled changes.

Disadvantages

- Extra resource will be required.
- Can be seen as an overhead by the customer.

Costs

- The implementation of effective configuration management and change control can be expensive in both team and management resources.

Improve Documentation

Description

- Create a logical system design on the basis of the physical system in use. Implementation may be done with an automatic documentation tool.

Benefits

- Standardisation.
- Logical design documentation is easier to maintain.

Disadvantage

- The bureaucrats can have a field day if not kept under control.

Costs

- This can be relatively cheap, although it is (in practice) often time consuming.

Do nothing

Description

- This implies implementing any minor changes under consideration with perhaps some redeployment of staff. This is basically only feasible on a system that is in good condition, or a system which is not business critical and will have a very short life span.

Benefits

- Cheapest.
- Consumes very little resources.
- By deferring change it is possible to await the arrival of new technologies.

Disadvantages

- Each change may degrade the system further.
- Increasing customer dissatisfaction.

- The system will get worse without you realising it.

- The chance of any recovery of the project is lost.

Costs

- Very low in the short term but they will be very high in the long term if you allow a sick project to get into the field.

6.4   PROCESS IMPROVEMENT

The problem with process improvement is that, usually, you see little short-term advantage. This is difficult to cope with, even when the project is a long-term venture. If the project itself is short term, there is strong temptation to go out and buy a tool from the Snake Oil Salesmen who are always waiting for people who don't want to take real medicine.

The effect on the project is similar to the effect of most of the snake oils (which contain a large proportion of alcohol)—they make you feel better in the short term but later you are poorer and have a terrible headache! If you apply a tool to the project without understanding the process your problems will get worse; the old saying still applies to software 'a fool with a tool is still a fool.'

So, what can you do?

The object here is to find the areas of the process where improvements will have most impact. If the process in use has been healthchecked or audited against ISO9000-3 (see Chapter 5 and Appendix 1) the main problem areas should be discernable from the audit results. If no form of audit has taken place, it is important to establish some key issues that need to be rectified. This can be done quite quicky, either by following the guidelines in this book or, simply, by listening to what the project team have to say.

Once you know the state of the process, if the recovery is to be sustainable, you need quick victories. The rule (again) is little and often .... and publish the successes. This last item is easy to do and frequently forgotten. As stated earlier, goals that can be achieved in short timescales are a great confidence and team builder. These goals have to be planned, achieved and celebrated to keep the momentum of recovery going.

We still need to ensure there in no relapse and that the basic hygiene of the project is sound. Steps should be taken to ensure that you learn from mistakes and do not make the same one again. One way of doing this is to install a working quality system that collects and collates project-meaningful records. The definition of a working quality system is one where the manual and the procedures are more important than the certificate. Again, simplicity is the keyword for success. Collecting and analysing the vital process indicators (e.g. % time spent in design review, average time to fix a fault, etc) is both straightforward and valuable.

6.5   A RECOVERY MODEL

In order to sustain the recovery of the project, a simple model can help. We propose one based on the Kolb Learning Circle (see Figure 6.1). This is very closely related to the Japanese approach. It consists of a circle (known as the virtuous circle) that, if correctly applied, gives a base for continuous process improvement.

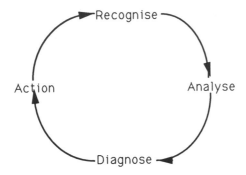

Figure 6.1   The RADAR learning cycle

In the case of project recovery you enter the circle at Recognition, as you should already have the uncomfortable experience of knowing that there is a problem you need to look into. The first step is to analyse the problem, drawing some conclusions from the vital few signs or measures that you collect. You then apply diagnostic techniques to find the root cause (and possible solutions) before drawing up an action plan. Then it is back to the recognise stage to find the next problem.

The second time round this circle is critical, as the object is to make changes quicker than the project is being changed by external events. So, again, we have to look for the targets that can be hit soon and hard to show the team and the customer that the project is recovering.

6.6   SUMMARY

This chapter has examined the kill or cure question that has to be resolved for any sick project. The main factor in this decision should be not the beauty, elegance or fun of the project but the solidity of its business case.

A number of alternative scenarios have been suggested for starting a recovery. Some are fairly dramatic, others very simple—the skill and challenge of recovery comes in deciding which is most appropriate on each occasion.

Whilst recognising that projects do get sick, it is also important to accept that ongoing health needs to be managed. This is covered in greater detail in the next chapter, but a basic model for ensuring continued project health is outlined here. A continual cycle passing through phases of Recognition, Analysis, Diagnosis and Action is used here as a framework for long-term project success.

In practice, all projects have an ongoing series of ills which can be (and often are) picked up on this sort of continuous improvement cycle. In the authors' experience, once a framework for improvement is put in place, the state of unrest in a problem project fuels the desire to improve and solutions come flooding out.

The next chapter takes some of the ideas put forward here and demonstrates how they relate to real projects. As always, the reality can be modelled on a theory of good practice, but all projects are unique and the medicine must match both the symptoms and the patient.

7
Recovery and Continued Health

The longest march starts with a single step

Mao Tse-tung

Armed with the guidelines and advice from earlier chapters, it should be fairly straightforward to locate and cure any project ailments. Unfortunately, project recovery is a complex and, often, long-term exercise that tests the nerve of most people. This chapter aims to illustrate just how the whole recovery process can actually work.

It is worth reinforcing at this point that recovery, like diagnosis, is not an exact science. Some projects 'reject' all attempts to bring them back on course. Others respond to some of the medicine selected but not to the complete prescription. Many projects do get better, though, as illustrated by the case study outlined here.

Recovery is not the end of the story, though. The ultimate aim in software projects should be continued good health. Even if a project has not been sick, regular checkups and screening are required to keep it healthy. If it has been sick and has been recovered then it is even more important to ensure that it does not slide back. A sad tale of what can—and does—go wrong during a recovery is given at the end of this chapter.

7.1 A TALE OF RECOVERY

The SAMBA project was originally conceived as a local system to control a collection of digital telephone exchanges. Shortly after the project had started to move through to specification and design, its scope was extended on the (perfectly reasonable) basis that the outline design would allow extra functions to be added. By the time the first releases were being implemented, the SAMBA system had grown from a local switch manager to an international network service management system.

This growth in scope while the project was under way brought with it several consequences. First, the project was elevated onto the list of mission critical initiatives. It had to succeed. Second, the number of people working on it grew. The original small team became, within the space of eight months, a project workforce of nearly a hundred people spread across three sites. Third, the target market changed. The original plans and choice of technology (a state of the art design architecture) began to look rather out of place.

This was the situation when the overall project management was changed in an attempt to speed delivery. A number of experienced project managers were introduced into the project and it was their fresh view that triggered the ensuing programme of recovery.

The symptoms

There were a number of warning signs that immediately struck the incoming project team, the main ones being:

- The customer was reticent to commit details of what the system should achieve. Requirements were elicited on a short-term, piecemeal basis rather than as logical steps towards an overall vision. The timescales for effective planning often exceeded that allowed by this limited definition of the end target.

- The software was being developed in advance of the hardware being available, and the specification for the hardware was yet to be fixed.

- Despite the fact that firm release dates had been promised to the customer, there was no release plan showing how those dates were to be achieved. The milestones that were shown in the project proposal (lodged with the project office, as required by the local quality procedures) focused only on internal events such as stage reviews.

- The project team were spending nearly all of their time fire-fighting. They were continually being bombarded with a combination of new requirements, interface changes and 'urgent' patch requests.

- There were no consistent configuration management procedures in place. An increasing amount of time was being wasted tracking down lost components and applying the right fixes to the wrong version of the system.

- Because of the pressure to deliver, the team leaders who should have been controlling the developments were having to help with implementation.

- The project manager was so busy making sure that the project administration was correctly set up[1] that he had little time to communicate the context and status of the project to the team. Also, the three team leaders at the different project sites talked to their own teams about the local issues but they did not communicate with each other on the overall project issues.

- As a follow on from the above, the teams had divergent and, often, out of date perceptions of what the project was all about and why it was important to the company.

In addition to the above points, there was an increasing concern within the teams that the project was not going to work. Critical information was being increasingly vested in a small number of experts and no-one really had a complete understanding of the overall system configuration.

Realisation that these problems existed was the first step in the recovery process. The next was admitting in the first major project review to both the customer and to the project teams the existence of the problems.

Although difficult, this simple act of admission got the recovery off to a flying start. The people working on the project saw that their managers were committed to delivering a reasonable product and were not slavedrivers aiming at impossible targets. The customer (having calmed down) had a much more realistic view of what could really be achieved.

Figure 7.1 illustrates the dramatic effect of announcing a major hiatus in project progress. The customer and supplier view of what is possible come

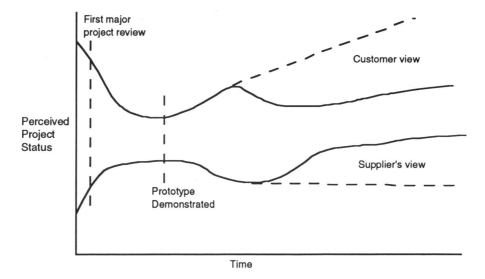

Figure 7.1   Managing expectations

---

[1] In practice, this involved a large amount of mandatory project description documentation, justification of project objectives and detailed financial accounting and forecasting.

closer together—a major contributor to project health. The continued management of expectation is an important part of recovery.

The next step was the plan for recovery.

The action plan

The course of treatment for this project was carefully put together. First the interfaces between the main functional teams were clearly defined. An agreed process map, showing what was delivered to whom, was drawn up as shown in Figure 7.2. This was crucial in allowing overall project priorities to be identified as it made clear, for the first time, the impact of local action on the project as a whole.

Next, the project priorities were identified and agreed. This process involved accepting that not *everything* could be high priority—some desirable features and actions had to be deferred. A key consequence of getting the overall project map drawn up was that it made clear when one person's vital issue would not impact the project over much. Also, it showed that a small matter for one area might have major impact elsewhere.

Along with the project map, a complete set of project risks was put together along with the action planned for each one. There was nothing fancy about this. Some codified and mutually agreed common sense plus a little forward planning yielded a valuable reference, as shown in Figure 7.3.

A picture was soon created of the strategic requirements for the project and the potential problems that needed to be borne in mind in achieving them. Initially the outlook covered the next three months. A later version (in

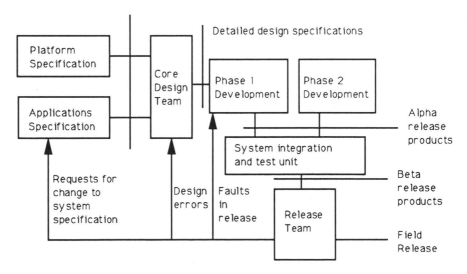

Figure 7.2   The overall project process map

Risk priority	Risk Id	Weeks on list	Description	Action
1	12	4	- Accommodation for demo	- Escalate
3	4	12	- Delivery of Circuits	- Reuse from other project
2	15	3	- Workstation upgrade needed	- Hire, then order new kit
3	27	new	- Contracts expire	- Renew asap
1	26	new	- No requirements for next stage	- Work on knowns, help reqs process
3	2	14	- Test scripts incomplete	- Schedule update
1	17	2	- Team unclear on plans	- Awayday planned

Figure 7.3 A simple project risk plan

less detail) extended over the next two years. This has to be set against the pre-recovery situation where the agreed outlook rarely extended beyond two weeks and where issues that could have been resolved with early action often escalated into major crises.

Once the above information was in a coherent format (and this took no more than two weeks to assemble and ten pages to express), it was shared with the team. A project review for the entire team was held. At this review, the way forward was outlined and comments on how best to get there invited. Quite apart from the useful ideas put forward (many of which were subsequently implemented) this was the first time that everyone on the project had met.

The third step in the recovery was getting on top of what had already been done. There was no intent to change (or even understand) what existed—simply to establish exactly what the component parts of the system were and how they fitted together. Following on logically from this, well defined configuration management procedures were introduced. For the first time, everyone on the project could identify exactly what they were working with.

As soon as the common naming conventions and filing practices were established, it became possible to specify the exact status of the system in terms of a baseline set of components. This level of traceability enabled some simple fault reporting measurements to be introduced and the more problematical components to be identified.

Having completed the above, it was possible to start the long-term recovery.

The recovery

The first recovery aim was to ensure that short-term pressures did not preclude change. An overall target was set for the amount of effort that would be allocated to strategic development and how much would be allowed for firefighting. Initially the split was set at 10/90, with the aim of moving down to 50/50 over the next six months and falling to 70/30 after two years.

The first move towards this aim was to take three people out of the implementation team They were asked to build an outline future release plan on the basis of known problems, project priorities and the above allocation of resources. This was accomplished within two weeks, whereupon these three formed the system release team. Their function was refined (this is illustrated in Figure 7.4) so that a firm grip could be kept on what was being delivered, what the outstanding problems were and where the new problems were coming from [KI84].

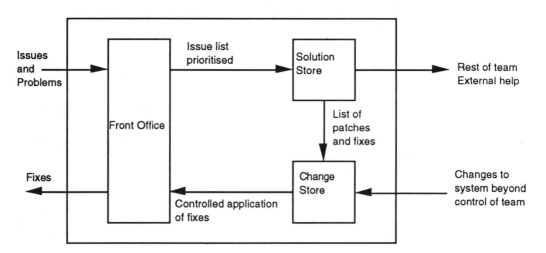

Figure 7.4   The release team role

A number of key measures were identified as part of the above setup:

- Overall times to fix a fault.

- Number of faults outstanding per module.

- Faults raised against each module.

- Likely source of fault.

All of these were collated for analysis at the weekly progress meetings. In practice, this meant no more than building a project release spreadsheet and database on a standard issue personal computer.

It soon became clear that there were a small number of particularly trouble-some modules. These were easily spotted as they had an increasing number of outstanding faults and, generally, longer than average times to fix. One of these was an ill-defined interface; another was traced back to an unclear requirement.

The former was cured by tying down the interface definition, the latter by rewriting that part of the system to be data driven instead of running to embedded information. The effort invested in re-engineering these two was repaid within a month through reduced maintenance [War89].

The next move in the recovery process was to establish an accurate and understandable system specification. This was to become an essential refer-ence point for future development. For illustration, part of this top-level sys-tem specification is shown in Figure 7.5. This was the first time that all of the various development teams saw how their work fitted into the project. As well as giving everyone on the project an idea of the context in which they were working, the specification provided a basis for a common set of test schedules to be built [LJP81]. The next move towards strategic project effort was to automate some of these test schedules by installing regression testers. Later, a redesign and reuse exercise was initiated. The project even got round to using the rigorous review technique described earlier in Chapter 5.

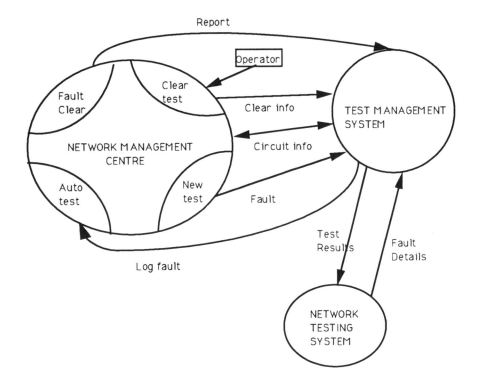

Figure 7.5   Simple process overview of system

Little by little the recovery was working.

The weekly project review meetings took action based on:

- progress against plans and overall specification

- statistics generated by the release team.

And they visited some of the design and release team meetings to gauge the coalface view of how the project was going.

This contrasts with previous meetings which had been a short-term reaction to that week's problems.

At the same time that the recovery process was being pursued, some new blood was introduced into the team. This also had significant effect.

The teams had previously been, typically, white males aged 25 to 35 with a computer science background. One older male ex-teacher, taken on as a specialist project administrator, had the planning documentation and reporting organised in no time—freeing up the project manager for his real job. And a young lady (also an ex-teacher) did wonders for application of common sense in the team by maintaining the risk register and driving the design reviews. In both cases the outlook and skill base of the team was widened to good effect.

In the final analysis, the recovery of this project was a major success. It took nearly a year before this was seen from the outside but, as stated at the start of this chapter, recovery can be a long and demanding process.

7.2   WHAT CAN GO WRONG DURING RECOVERY?

Not all recoveries work. Sometimes the wrong symptoms are diagnosed, sometimes the wrong cures are applied. Even when all the right steps are taken and the recovery is well planned things can go wrong. This section looks at a few of the more common sources of terminal project decline.

Silver bullets

Perhaps the most common pitfalls in any recovery programme are the 'silver bullet' traps. These are the attractive but misguided notions that adding people or technology to the project will cure everything.

The futility of throwing more and more people at a problem was recognised in the early days of software development by Brookes [Bro75]. Despite this, many projects since then have been killed off (often in spectacular fashion) by the very medicine that was meant to cure them. When it comes to introducing new people into a project, there is a law of diminishing returns. It takes time to contribute—some for the new blood to learn, some for the old hands to teach. A managed growth of effort is a lot more credible than a gung-ho call for a doubling of programmers 'to deliver it in half the time'!

Just as new people are no panacea, so too is new technology. The rapid introduction, and subsequent mothballing, of many CASE tools in the late 1980s is a good example of this. There are two underlying problems prevalent when new technology is brought in.

First is the mistaken belief that it will have instant impact. In practice, new tools take time to learn and set up properly. It is usually months before teething problems (e.g. getting printers working, etc) are resolved and the tools are being used to good effect.

The second, and more serious, problem is that tools are sometimes used in place of, rather than to support, a defined process. In this case they do no more than automate the decline and fall of the project. There are plenty of well established guides to good software engineering practice [GEC86, NCC87] Basic technology (e.g. electronic mail, configuration management tools, etc) is necessary. Anything else should be viewed with suspicion.

The one-off solution

Even if sensible plans are put in place to start with, continuous monitoring is required. Recovery is a management exercise that requires many balanced decisions to be taken. There is no way that even the best of recovery plans will just run to completion.

For instance, an ailing project may require no more than some tightening of its quality control processes. When the required procedures are introduced, they will be appropriate to the job in hand. If left unattended, though, they are likely to become more of a problem than an asset. Many projects grind to a halt through too many so-called quality checks. The very procedures that established control earlier in a project can become an end in themselves and constrain rather than enable.

Be wary of plans and processes, established early in recovery, that remain unchanged. A viable recovery plan needs to avoid getting bogged down in too much detail—a clear view of the way ahead is essential, fine tuning can come later. Also, it is vital that direction setting comes from within the team, not from external bodies which can add on additional complications. External influences have their role, but recovery must be owned by the project team.

Open kimono

Recovery should not be a witchhunt. If it is known that blame is being apportioned more time will be spent proving innocence (or non-participation) than moving the project forward. Nothing demotivates more than this sort of atmosphere and it become attractive to do nothing on the grounds that all action carries risk of retribution [DML87]. Initiative becomes anathema, the new Jobsworth (see Chapter 4) is bred and the project stalls.

Perhaps the only exception to the no-blame rule is the Jonah or 'bad apple' in the team who will not accept change. If one or more people continually reject the required medicine, they need to be taken off any critical paths and, ultimately, off the project altogether.

The remote customer

A nail (or more accurately, a whole bag of nails) in the coffin of many recovering projects is lack of customer committment. In the absence of a focus for delivery, projects can easily veer towards producing, verbatim, what the specification calls for. And this often fails to satisfy the real need.

Real projects rarely have a correct and comprehensive set of requirements to start with. Continual refinement and interpretation of the initial statement of requirements is usually needed to deliver a system that does what the customer *actually* wants. This can only be achieved if the customer is involved in the recovery process and is clear why the project needs to succeed.

There are other ways in which recovery can go astray but those outlined above are by far the most prevalent terminators of good intent. The basic message is that common sense and continuing attention is called for. Radical actions, grand plans and macho management may appear dynamic but, more often than not, they cannot be sustained [Jay87]. Recovery is a marathon, not a sprint.

7.3   CONVALESCENCE AND CONTINUED GOOD HEALTH

Our last story is a brief tale of a project that was bought under control and then lost its way again. The sole reason for running through this account is to illustrate that projects need continued attention if they are to remain healthy. Even the best can go wrong if left to its own devices for too long.

The Essay project started life as a joint industry–university research collaboration. The idea was to explore the possibilities of generating software automatically from pictorial representations. The work was innovative and, at the time, well ahead of anything commercially available. The project wandered, though. There were plenty of interesting prototype features and functions but no real hard edge to the project.

The recovery of the project was initiated by a new team leader who had recently worked in an area that would have made good use of Essay, had it been a reliable, usable product. The ensuing recovery programme followed much the same lines (on a smaller scale) as the SAMBA project. A clear set of project targets were put in place. A phased release plan for the product was established and the necessary product release and support teams were put in place. For a year or so, all went well. A series of good quality enhancements to the basic system were produced. At the height of the recovery, the Essay product set was easily the most sophisticated on the market. The developments in the pipeline promised to keep it that way for the forseeable future.

It was at this stage that things started to go wrong. The first sign that all was not well was the quiet but discernable voice of discontent from the project teams. They were delivering good technical products but sales were flat—if anything, declining.

This situation continued for some six months. The quality of the system continued to improve but sales did not move. An increasing amount of time and effort was invested in promoting the product. This often meant diverting the developers onto demonstration and promotional activities, a role they did not relish.

The forced coupling of the development and sales teams soon unearthed some real problems. At an operational level it was clear that the two had not been communicating very effectively for some time. What was being sold was not what was being developed. More worrying were the developers' views on the system marketing plans. Their observation was that the people actually using the system had bought it, primarily, as a general purpose drawing package, not as a code generation tool. The projected sales in the Essay business plan relied on major sales to code producers. It soon became clear that this was not going to happen and further development effort was cut. By this stage all of the energy and enthusiasm in the project had evaporated.

The project was put on ice and was gracefully wound down within the year. In retrospect, many of those who worked on the project considered the product to be too far ahead of its time. Five years on, similar (but technically less sophisticated) tools began to take off in the marketplace. If handled with more liaison between sales and development it could have capitalised on the five-year head start on the competition and continued as a leader in its field.

7.4 PRESSURES AND MOTIVATIONS

In the heat of battle it can be easy to overlook the obvious. Hopefully the stories, symptoms and cures outlined here will help. But it is important to be aware of the pressures and motivations of all of the people in the project.

In the last part of this chapter, we look at the context in which one of the key players in software projects, the project manager, operates. This is intended simply to illustrate the various pressures and motivations that need to be balanced. Figure 7.6 shows where the primary interfaces to project managers are and what each one expects them to deliver.

Much of what has been explained previously covers how these competing (and often conflictling) demands and expectations can be reconciled. There is one further point, though. This is that no project can be healthy unless there is give and take between all of the players. If the 'boss' in Figure 7.6 applies too much pressure, someone else suffers. Imbalances work to the detriment of the overall project and all players need to be sensitive to this. The wider the project team, the more likely this is to come about. And this is

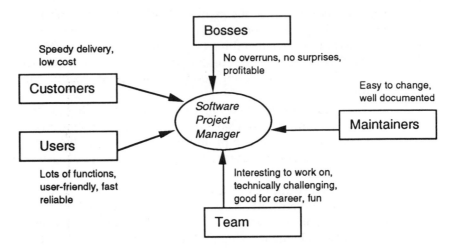

Figure 7.6   The motivations of the people involved in the software project

often apparent simply by looking at an organisation chart or talking to the people.

Driving forward with a project recovery is not easy and the project manager has to strike a balance between team involvment and external pressures. This is a difficult balance to achieve and an important one to understand. It has been suggested here that egoless management is the most appropriate style—trying to establish a balanced approach to the people and project needs without using high profile mangement techniques. The authors' experience is that this style can, and does, work. However, this should be tempered by the recognition that there are times when a more authoritarian approach is required of the project manager.

In the final analysis, it is down to the project manager to strike an appropriate balance, After all, it is the project manager who shoulders the majority of the blame for a failed project. There are, however, a number of levers that the project manager has available:

- *Formal authority.* This is provided by the position and status of the project team. On occasions, we have seen the customer use this to assist the project manager to achieve the required changes.

- *Control of resources.* The ability to exercise control of specialist resources (test facilities, system analysts, transmission capacity, etc) can be used constructively to bring about change.

- *Organisation.* Established processes and practices can be used to force change and this has a place in project recovery.

- *Control of decision processes.* This is linked to formal authority. The project manager has control over the information that is vested within the project and how it is used.

- *Boundary management.* The project manager is in the 'privileged' position of being at the centre of Figure 7.6. This brings with it a natural focus of information. Care need to be exercised in using the position sensibly.

- *Technology control.* Sometimes, even simple or mundane items such as new workstations help to generate leverage for change.

- *Alliances and informal networks.* These are a significant source of power, both internal to and external to the project.

With careful use of these levers, many an ailing project can be put back on track.

7.5 SUMMARY

The recovery of a sick project is rarely easy. It often requires dedicated effort over a considerable period of time. This chapter has looked at some typical project recoveries, but it is vital to realise that each project has its own particular problems and each customer has their own set of concerns and aspirations. There is no silver bullet.

The inappropriate use of medicine at the wrong time or for the wrong symptoms can lead to disaster. Attention needs to be paid at all times to the ongoing health of the project and the effects of any corrective action employed. However, there are a number of key pointers to help move a project from the sick stage through into a practical recovery phase:

- *Gain recognition.* Make sure that everyone realises that the project needs attention to restore it to a fit and healthy condition that will deliver to the customer's aspirations and leave the team able to continue into the future.

- *Establish a practical view.* Find out what needs to be done in practice, not just theory. Develop a short-term plan as soon as possible but also ensure that the overall picture of where the project is heading is built up and agreed.

- *Recognise the key risks.* Write them down, track them and lay down some plans for dealing with them. Attack both the effect and the root cause if you can.

- *Strive for consensus.* Accept that, at times, a dictatorial approach is required (especially to drive through initial changes) but aim to build a plan with the help and agreement of the rest of the people on the project.

- *Work with the team.* They often know best what is required. They have a depth and breadth of knowledge that should not be ignored. Be open to suggested courses of action.

- *Avoid explosive expansion.* Resist the temptation to bring more and more people on to the team. Evolve by all means but a single team of much more than 12 can get out of hand, as can growth in excess of 10% per month.

- *Manage team interactions.* Remove people who persistently resist change. Try to keep a balance of personalities within the team—this can be as valuable as technical skill.

- *Keep the people well informed.* Let people know why things are as they are. Make sure that the team see why decisions have been taken and that the customer's expectations are realistically managed.

Whilst the above list is not prescriptive or, indeed, exhaustive, it does provide a framework for the needs of the project during a phased and managed recovery. The balance of all of these requirements at the same time is what most well motivated and clearly focused project teams seem to be able to do.

It does not all happen at once, though, nor is recovery a short-term fix. Long-term dedicated effort and committment is the root of all successful recovered projects.

REFERENCES

[Bro75] Brookes F (1975) *The Mythical Man Month: Essays on Software Engineering* Addison-Wesley

[DML87] DeMarco T and Lister T (1987) *Peopleware* Dorset House

[GEC86] General Electric Company (1986) *Software Engineering Handbook* McGraw-Hill 1986

[Jay87] Jay A (1987) *Management and Machiavalli* Hutchison Business

[KI84] Kling R and Iacono S (1984) The control of information systems developments after implementation *Commun.ACM* vol 27 no 12 pp1218–1226

[LJP81] Peters, L J (1981) *Software Design: Methods and Techniques* Yourdon Press

[NCC87] National Computing Centre (1987) *The STARTS Guide*, Volume 1, 2nd Edition

[War89] Warden R H (1989) Software re-engineering, a practical approach *Proc. 1st Int. Conf. on Software Maintenance Tools (London, June 1989)*

8

The Well Project Clinic

*This is not the end, not even the beginning of the end
but it is the end of the beginning*

Winston Churchill

In previous chapters we have outlined many of the problems that bedevil software projects and some viable solutions to them. In this last chapter we aim to bring together these anecdotes, techniques and guidelnes to provide an outline for monitoring the condition of the project—a well project clinic. This will consist of a basic set of parameters that, if monitored regularly and kept in balance, will keep a project healthy.

The prime user of the well project clinic would be the project manager—the very simplicity of its construction acknowledges the limited time available to this person. Its usefulness is broader, though, and all team members have relevant input. It may also be useful if the customer either has access to or develops their own version of these project monitors

In operation, the idea is to match the doctor's use of charts that record readings of the patient's vital signs and symptoms, such as temperature, blood pressure and bowel function. The object is to list the metrics gathered as an indication of the overall health and hence to indicate the effect the treatment is having.

If you step back and look at the progress of a software project from the three basic standpoints of people, process and product, each has one or more distinct telltale indicators. Together they provide a clear picture of overall health.

If we continue the analogy and monitor these indicators, it becomes possible to identify early signs of project sickness before they turn into an illness requiring major surgery. Only minimal medication is then required to keep the project well.

But all these measures must be taken regularly, just like the patient's temperature, and they should only be used as indicators—not direct measures to beat the team with or categorical attestations of project quality. .

The aim of the next few pages is to build up the project manager's equivalent of the car dashboard described in Chapter 6—something to give the project manager an indication of the health of his project, as illustrated in Figure 8.1. The data gathered to provide the visual display is a mix of fairly standard project, quality or financial indicators.

The data for this should be collected in line with some form of standard so that the results can be reused locally and, perhaps, across business units. One such benchmark is the European Quality Award, which details a range of assessment criteria covering processes, people and products. A small sub-set of these will enable you to regularly assess a project. We now suggest what this sub-set should cover.

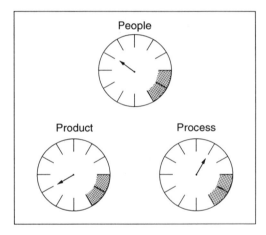

Figure 8.1   The project dashboard

8.1   PEOPLE PARAMETERS

People, as well as projects, move through phases—early enthusiasm, midterm complacency, eventual disillusionment, and many others. In order to draw on the strong points in each phase, it is important to track them.

There are three key areas that can be monitored:

1 - team morale

2 - management action.

3 - customer expectation.

Team morale

This is a subjective measure but none the less valuable for its subjectivity. When you choose to use it as a yardstick, care needs to be taken in accounting for local circumstances such as the size of the team, etc. Bearing this in mind, the first of our dashboard instruments can be put together with inputs on:

- Sick leave (any more than two days per person per annum would merit a negative morale rating).

- Length of lunch breaks (anything over 45 minutes away from the workplace would usually give a negative rating).

- Number of ideas from the team that have been implemented on the project (the breakeven is about one per person per week).

- Number of social/charity events per month (for a team of ten, one is average and attendance should be about 80%).

A usable morale rating can readily be derived from these inputs. The weight given to each varies from project to project, but a reasonable morale metric can be assembled with a little local effort.

There are other factors that tell a lot about morale. Some are indirect such as the number of jokes at meetings or the level of attendance at reviews, planning meetings, etc. Some are direct, the most straighforward being so-called 'employee attitude' surveys. These can add or modify the morale metric derived here but, in both cases, they are based on perception or theory rather than actual behaviour.

Management action

Now that we have one part of the dashboard, we can start to add complementary information. In contrast with the 'soft' measure of morale, there is the very hard measure of time spent on the project. In particular, the amount of time spent managing the project (as opposed to contributing to the end product) is particularly telling. Figure 8.2 shows a typical graph of management effort being expended on the project against the project plan budget. In the graph there is clearly an increase in work up to the decision to put a recovery process in place, a further increase during the first phase of the recovery and then a decrease once the recovery is underway. This simple graph is very telling and gives a clear picture of the status of the project. Again, this is a very simple measure to make but it is both useful and difficult to obscure.

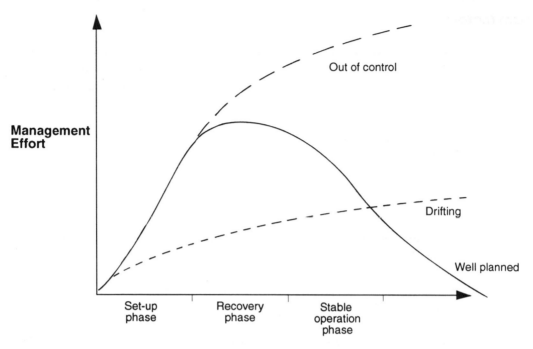

Figure 8.2   Measurement effort against time

Customer expectation

This is the last of the people part of the dashboard. In contrast with the two parameters described above, customer satisfaction *has* to be based on perception rather than actuals. Nonetheless, it can be measured in a standard way through the use of perception surveys that seek to establish customer ratings for various aspects of the supplier's performance. The key aspects that should be given a customer rating (e.g. marks out of ten) are:

- Value for money
- Understanding of customer's business
- Level of project reporting
- Accuracy of project reporting
- Contribution to customer's business
- Timeliness of deliverables.

Quite apart from giving the customer confidence that they are being listened to, the customer satisfaction survey provides a useful reference for the future. Figure 8.3 illustrates what goes on to the dashboard.

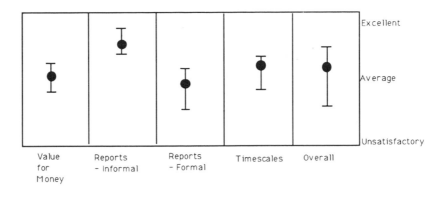

Figure 8.3 Customer satisfaction survey results

Together, the three measures described above give a good picture of the people side of the project. This is the most difficult to establish. Next comes the process.

8.2 PROCESS INDICATORS

The software development process has been documented in many ways, from the sequential waterfall model to the evolutionary spiral or snail. The choice of which to follow is dependent upon the type of customer, the nature of the project and the practice within the team. Whichever model is adopted, there are key criteria against which effectiveness can be judged.

To a large extent, these have already been covered—and further detail is given in Appendix 1. The only point that really needs to be made here is that the process indicator should be based on what is really happening. The healthcheck technique outlined in Chapter 5 is an ideal candidate for the process indicator on the dashboard. Others, such the SEI assessment, can be used but the healthcheck gives a good current picture of how well internal processes are being run.

A secondary indicator in this category is the deathcycle, described in Chapter 4. The key parameters to be recorded in this are the actual spend on the project, the dates when the product is to be sold and the incoming revenue from the sale(s). The predicted marketing window for the project can also be monitored. The cash flow can then be tracked by plotting actual expenditure. If the predicted area under the curve ever becomes larger then you are falling into a loss-making situation and urgent action is required.

Together with the healthcheck, this gives a picture of internal project effectiveness and of external project value. The dashboard is nearing completion.

One caveat in this section is that process indicators based on conformance to a QMS are not very stable. Unlike the healthcheck and deathcycle, QMS measures are linked to the process definition rather that the project target. So using this on the dashboard can be rather like following a map based on what the terrain *should* be like, not what it *is* like.

8.3   PRODUCT INDICATORS

The above measures are to a large extent soft measures. They need to be underpinned with some hard product-based metrics. The object here is simple—to gather metrics that are of use and, more importantly, to use those measures as a basis for improving future quality in the project.

The range of measures that can be used has been well covered in Chapter 5, which introduced a product assessment lifecycle, and in Appendix 2 which gives details of a range of product meures. For the dashboard, there are probably two relevant indicators:

- Number of faults per unit time per release
- Number of outstanding requests for change.

Both give a view of whether a situation is getting better or worse. They have to be tempered with other project factors (such as rates of usage, number of released systems, etc) but applied with common sense they give a good indication of end product quality. Furthermore, they help to locate areas where more measures could usefully be made.

Putting together the people, process and product indicators suggested here, we get a final dashboard, as illustrated in Figure 8.4.

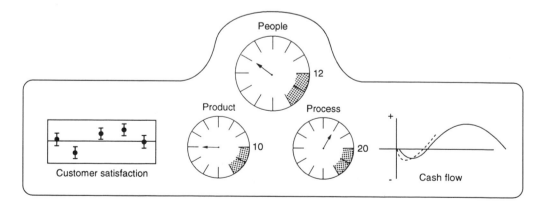

Figure 8.4   The indicators on the project dashboard.
Typical parameters are: people: average days sick per month + % staff turnover; process: % late milestones per month; product: % change in fault reports per month

The individual indicators may change, the weightings given to particular aspects can be varied but the important thing is that the above diagram shows, at a glance, the health of the project. This is the first step to finding, and curing, any underlying ills. To achieve this in any real situation, there may have to be more information and the balance between practicality and usefulness would have to be carefully considered. But the basic equipment is there—the rest is up to the people who run it.

8.4 FINAL THOUGHTS

One thing that should be clear from the stories earlier in this book is that software projects can go terribly wrong. They are traditionally seen as difficult to manage. But, at the same time, it is apparent that the same mistakes are being made again and again. Also, similar remedies are being found to correct the mistakes. In short, software project management is coming of age!

This is an opportunity. To date it has been the case that large projects could only realistically be carried out as in-house developments. The increasing globalisation of many large companies means that they are beginning to find out how to manage the delivery of software projects with much more control. It is becoming possible to broaden the base of the team—and still keep the project healthy. Companies that were once constrained by their software skillbase are learning how to grow the vital resource to make this happen—the modern software project manager, a new addition to the long line of professional engineering managers

This book has explored the healthy project. It has taken a broad look at what makes a software project tick, from the people who participtate to the code that is produced. There are ways, means, measures and methods to ensure that they all converge on the desired end. As the call for software-rich systems inexorably rises, so will the call for people who can make the people, the process and the product work in harmony.

Appendix 1

Quality Management Systems

Obviously the obvious is not that obvious

James Thurber

This appendix looks at the most basic aspect of process control—the introduction of a quality management system (QMS). Before we move on to the practical details of developing, installing and instilling a QMS, a little background, is presented.

The history of quality management systems can be traced back as far as the Pharaohs in Egypt, when funerary goods had to be approved by the Superintendent of the Necropolis and bore his mark.

The roots of modern quality standards stem from the Industrial Revolution. In the UK the revolution was fuelled by a desire to supply cheap goods to the ever expanding empire.

The emphasis on quality over quantity came from the USA where the military and settlers in the expanding west demanded guns with interchangeable parts. Until this time, guns were handmade on a one-off basis and hence replacement parts were also handmade by highly skilled and experienced gunsmiths. There was at this time a shortage of these skills in the USA. This led to what was known as the American system of manufacture, a method of high precision mass production.

The American system of manufacture was developed using, as its base, automatic control with an unskilled immigrant workforce from Europe employed as machine loaders and watchers. These machines had to be set up and their adjustment monitored by highly skilled tradesmen. This can be considered as quality inspection throughout the process. This form of mass production was also responsible for the introduction of productivity measurement, time and motion studies and the division of the labour force into management, skilled tradesmen and unskilled labourers.

The skilled tradesmen were responsible for the inspection and hence quality of the production process. As the size of companies increased and the complexity of the goods produced also increased, this inspection process was passed from one tradesman to the next down the manufacturing line.

The next step was the introduction of inspectors who were independent of the manufacturing operation who would look at the goods and return any that were defective for rework or as scrap.

The first successful attempt to document and standardise this process was an American military specification MIL-Q-9858A in 1963. The development of standards then followed the diagram shown in Figure A1.1. The instruments of change are illustrated for clarification.

NATO set up the Allied Quality Assurance Publication (AQAP) as a derivative of the US MIL standard. The UK, despite being a member of NATO, set up its own defence standard DEFSTAN 05/21, 05/24, and 05/29 again in a similar format to both AQAP and US MIL standards. The need for a commercial industry standard in the UK was met by the British Standards Institute, who produced BS5750 in 1979. This was further refined until 1987 when the International Standards Organisation produced ISO9000 which was based (almost verbatim) on BS5750.

The ISO9000 consists of four parts ISO9001, 9002, 9003, 9004:

ISO9000 - Quality Management and Quality Assurance Standards—
    Guidelines for Selection and Use.

ISO9001 - Quality Systems—Model for Quality Assurance in
    Design/Development, Production, Installation and Servicing.

ISO9002 - Quality Systems—Model for Quality Assurance in Production
    and Installation.

ISO9003 - Quality Systems—Model for Quality Assurance in Final
    Inspection and Test.

ISO9004 - Quality Management and Quality System Elements—Guidelines.

The ISO9000 standards have been adopted into the national standards systems of most manufacturing countries world wide In the European Community it is known as Euronorme EN29000-1987.

Basically ISO9000 is all about documenting and standardising the process, just as the gunsmiths in the USA did. It represents the current best practice in management and control when applied to software production.

We, in the software industry, are at the same stage as the gun manufacturers of the USA before industrialisation—a few gurus who make very good systems and the rest who often deliver poor quality software, late. Will history repeat itself?

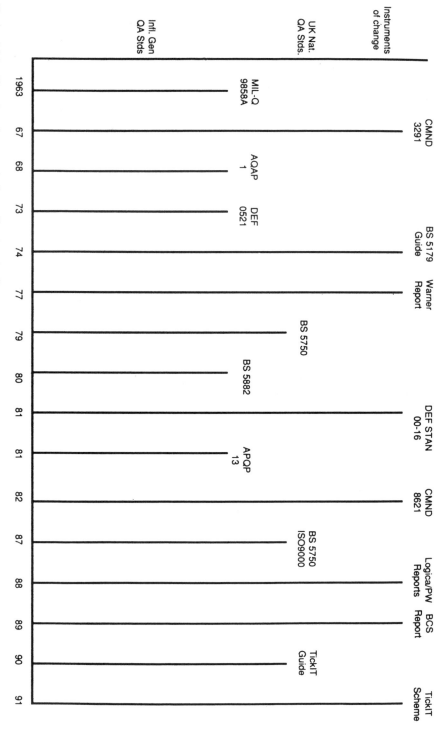

Figure A1.1 The development of quality standards

It looks very much like it with the quest for metrics, formal methods, etc. We are now at the stage of injecting quality into the production of software and are attempting to move to quality assurance. This is where the quality management systems come into their own. Before describing ISO9000 in detail, we will attempt to answer some common questions and outline the benefits of having a QMS in place for a software project.

A1.1   A BRIEF GUIDE TO THE ISO9000 QUALITY SYSTEMS

What is ISO9000?
- ISO 9000 is concerned with the quality assurance of functional organisation capabilities (e.g. the software production process).

Why is it needed?
- There must be a basic plan for quality. It does not just happen. This is just one way of continuously meeting the requirements and expectations of customers.

What is a quality plan?
- A document setting out the specific quality practices resources and activities relevant to a particular product, service contract or project.

What is quality assurance?
- The assurance to the customer that effective procedures exist to ensure all requirements will be met and the product resulting from the total engineering process will be satisfactory.
  This is an offical definition, a better one is: quality assurance is the business of ensuring that good software is not the result of good luck but the inevitable reward for good management practice.

Who does it affect and what are their responsibilities?
- Anyone associated with planning, sales, training, supply, design, manufacture, inspection, testing, customer services, maintenance, engineering, field service—in short, almost everyone.
  The responsibilities of the customer, people involved in the process and the supplier are shown in Figure A1.2.

What does ISO 9000 require?
- The following pages outline the different requirements which, if complied with, will mean the company is operating a good quality management system.

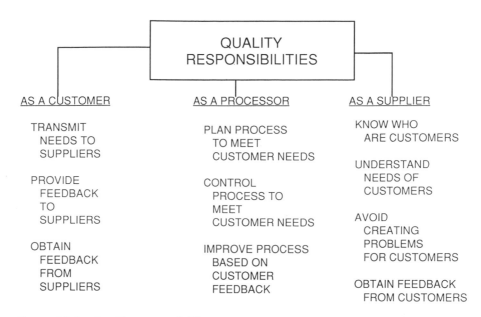

Figure A1.2   Quality responsibilities

A1.2   THE PARTS OF ISO9001

The ISO9001 document is a generic model for a quality management system. The same document can be used to build a quality system in almost any product or service. To make ISO9001 applicable to the software industry, supporting documentation has been produced by the Internarional Standards Organisation. The guidelines for the application of ISO9001 to the development, supply and maintenance of software have been given the confusing number of ISO9000-3 (note the dash). All of the 20 parts of the ISO9001 standard still apply, but to help the understanding of each section a short guide (with comments) is included.

Requirement 1: Management Responsibility/Quality policy

There must be a definite programme for quality. The policy must be communicated and understood throughout the company. Management must regularly review the whole quality system to ensure its continued effectiveness and conformance to ISO9000. There must be effective management for quality with all responsibilities clearly defined in writing and sufficient resources to do the job.

We must have management...
With assigned authority...
Responsibility...

Obvious really! ... Just good management?
Now...getting down to detail...

Requirement 2: Quality system

All the systems and processes that directly or indirectly affect the quality of our product and services must be documented.

The documentation must be practical, current, complete and effectively controlled. It must also correspond to what really happens.

It is essential that we all know what we are supposed to do.
Documentation is the foundation of all good working practices.

Requirement 3: Contract review

We must ensure that:

(a)   we know what customer requirements are;
(b)   those requirements are documented and reviewed;
(c)   any changes to requirements are resolved;
(d)   we are able to meet requirements;
(e)   we have customer agreement.

Contracts and orders must be reviewed to ensure we continue to meet their requirements.
Customers must receive the products and services specified.

Requirement 4: Design control

A requirement aimed to ensure the finished design of products or services meets those needs specified by the customer.

Design is the foundation of quality. There is a need to plan and review system structure and function at an early stage.

Requirement 5: Document control

People need to know what they are required to do. Therefore, working practices must be documented, up to date, controlled and readily available. Obsolete documents should be removed promptly from use.

Are we up to date? Are we all using the same versions of the documentation? A vital part of configuration management.

Requirement 6: Purchasing

Materials, parts, and service that are bought from suppliers must be fit for purpose, meet our quality requirements, and be controlled. Purchase specifications must be clearly written so that a supplier knows where they stand and knows what is wanted—exactly.

The aim is to purchase only goods and services that are of the appropriate quality. This requirement also includes vendor appraisal and assessment of sub-contractors.

Requirement 7: Purchaser-supplied product

The customer may supply materials to be used on their jobs. Such materials must be securely stored and methods used to prevent deterioration or loss.

Look after your own and other people's property.

Requirement 8: Product identification and traceability

At any time it is important to know what any item is. What it belongs to. At what stage it is. What stages it has already completed. What was used to build it. Where parts came from and who did what to it. Once an item has been built, it is important we know where it goes. Where appropriate, there must be forward and backward traceability.

If an item goes wrong at any time, its history tells us what to do to prevent further failures. Large software systems have many components; it is essential to be able to put the right ones together.

Requirement 9: Process control

Production and installation must occur under controlled conditions. Employees must know what to do and the standards required. Controls should exist to ensure that only good quality products are provided. The operation may be complex, it might need special checks, additional instructions, special training and qualifications. Adequate work instructions, and standards to be met, should be written down to ensure work is done correctly with suitable tools, parts, methods, specifications, etc.

Consistent quality requires controlled processes.

A work instruction is always required, if the absence of one would affect quality.

Work instructions should be easily understood, practical, short, to the point,... and used.

Requirement 10: Inspection and testing

Products must be inspected or verified, and pass the acceptance criteria when being received, worked on, and prior to dispatch. Any products not conforming to these standards must be segregated so that corrective action can be carried out. Records should be kept for inspection work done in each stage.

Ensure that the final product meets all of the specifications. This is just verification, validation and testing of the software product by another name.

Requirement 11: Inspection measuring and test equipment

Equipment used for checking or testing of a product must be capable of accurately performing those functions.
It is also required that:

- All testing and measuring equipment is identified.

- records show the frequency of calibration.

- procedures for calibration exist and that calibration is traceable to recognised standards, eg BS5781.

- instructions exist on how to deal with products that have been checked using equipment which subsequently fails calibration.

This is not as important in software development, but becomes more important in systems development.

Requirement 12: Inspection and test status

When any product moves through a process its status must be obvious. This can be achieved by using cards, labels, records, physical location or other suitable means. Only products which pass the required tests are to be used or dispatched and should indicate who carried out the checks at each stage.

Distinguish between inspected and uninspected...good and bad. This is version control and just part of good configuration management.

Requirement 13: Control or non-conforming products

Even in the best systems things go wrong...the product doesn't conform... scrap is made. When this happens the product must be identified and segregated. Precise procedures must be established to rework the material or to dispose of it as appropriate. Above all, defective material or products must not be allowed to become mixed with good products.

Reducing scrap and the need for rework increases efficiency. Do we have scrap software? We definitely have too much rework.

Requirement 14: Corrective action

All procedures, processes and products need to be monitored and reviewed to ensure constant delivery of quality.

Any non-conformance to standards must be documented, analysed, the cause identified and corrective action taken to avoid a re-occurence.

This is a constant process and involves everyone. Customer complaint handling is also part of this corrective action. A major theme of this book is that past problems and difficulties should be documented so that they can be watched for and, hopefully, avoided in future projects.

Requirement 15: Handling storage, packaging and delivery

Products must be handled carefully to prevent damage. They must be stored in appropriately secure and/or controlled areas. All packaging must be to an adequate standard to prevent damage or deterioration to products whilst in storage or delivery.

Handle with care! A specific point for the software project is that a secure archive needs to be provided—84% of companies that have a fire in their computer room fold within four years of the fire.

Requirement 16: Quality records

Quality records must be maintained so we can demonstrate our level of achievement against required standards and hence prove the effectiveness of the quality system. All records must be legible, easily retrieved and methods employed to prevent deterioration or loss.

Records are the proof of achievement and provide the trail for finding errors to enable the process to be improved. Examples of quality records are review follow-up action list and audit corrective action list.

The importance of records will not need to be emphasised to anyone who has lost a key piece of information.

Requirement 17: Internal quality audits

The internal quality assurance auditors carry out impartial independent assessments and reviews. These are to check whether processes and procedures are still pertinent, effective and meet requirements. Timely corrective action should be identified where required.

Are we as good as we think we are? If not, find out what is wrong and fix it!

Requirement 18: Training

For employees to perform tasks satisfactorily and meet the required standards, they must be shown the correct methods and techniques to use. Appropriate training shall be provided and future needs identified. Records of this training and of any skills attained must be kept.

You should document both on and off the job training as well as experience. There should be a plan of any further training required.

Requirement 19: Servicing

Where servicing of equipment is a requirement, it must be well specified, carried out by adequately trained personnel and within agreed timescales.

Servicing done well, on time, by adequately trained staff leads to happy satisfied customers.

Requirement 20: Statistical techniques

Checking or testing the acceptability of products and processes can be done, using appropriate tools and techniques, on a sample basis, but the sample must be representative of the whole. Records must be maintained in order to identify trends and assist in forecasting.

We do not yet have any universally accepted metrics that can be used to predict or quantify software. There are two main types of software development measurements—the product and process metrics. These should be collected within the project management system used for the development. The object is to produce accurate, repeatable and accepted measures—see the main text for recommended measures and the remaining appendices for how to collect them.

We have been through the basics of the ISO9000 standard which provides the international standard for software quality management systems.

The installation of an effective QMS is not a straighforward matter. The remainder of this appendix provides an outline QMS and some guidelines for its introduction.

A1.3   MANAGING A QMS

It cannot be stressed too much that the management of a QMS should be a people issue

If the actions and reactions, of all staff, become *truly* quality driven then expensive failures and reworks can be drastically reduced or even eliminated. Too often quality is treated as a technical problem and technical fixes are applied, which do not work. An effective quality management system is necessarily people based. It needs to contain procedures and prescribed activities but the necessary prerequisite is that people apply the available technology in a sensible way. From past experience the pitfalls of a QMS are usually people related.

The starting point for any quality system is a clear management policy stating why the system exists. Any policy which puts assessment to ISO9001 as its primary objective is not satisfactory. The policy must state the reasons for having a quality system in terms of the organisation's business. The QMS is, in effect, part of the corporate strategy.

An example of a quality policy is as follows:

'The unit will provide competitive products and services which fully meet the agreed requirements of our internal and external clients. Products and services will be delivered:

- to specification, first time

- on time, every time.

All staff are personally responsible for the quality of their own work and work done under their supervision.

All work done will be to the appropriate standards and will comply with the department's quality management system.

The quality management system will:

- satisfy the quality policy

- add value to the business

- comply with the requirements of ISO9001'.

Given a policy framed like this it is possible, easy even, to define the scope and content of a quality system to satisfy it.

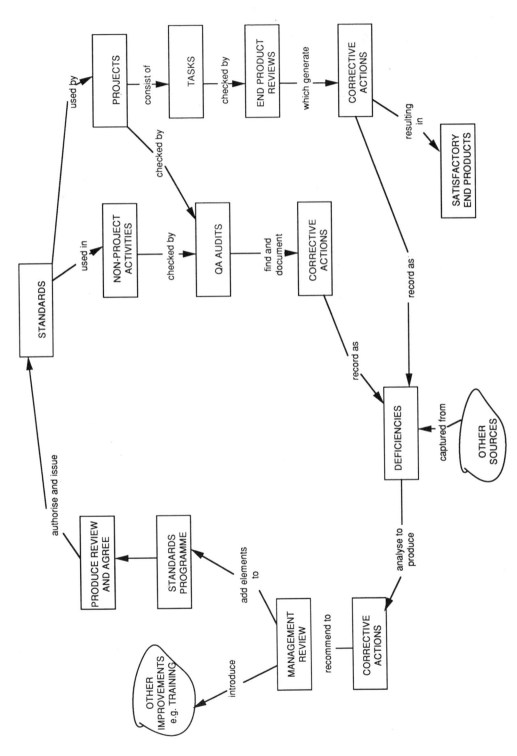

Figure A1.3 A view of a real QMS in operation

Figure A1.3 contains many important features of a QMS; the main ones are explained below.

QA audits

QA Audits examine all aspects of projects at the time of the audit. They should be conducted by people with considerable interpersonal skills and sensitivity. The audit report should add value to the auditees and line managers and, hence should give a balanced view of the project rather than being limited to statements of deficiencies. Follow-up audits should be conducted to ensure that corrective actions have been implemented in a reasonable timescale.

End product reviews

The technical quality of a project as a whole is determined by the quality of its end products. The basic quality control mechanism for most tasks is the review. Therefore every end product needs to be reviewed in an appropriate manner.

Reviews must be formally documented, with all corrective actions clearly recorded. They are not complete until all corrective actions have been undertaken and checked. Review documentation is essential evidence of quality control and must be retained, at least for the duration of the project. There are three main end types of product reviews used in software—inspection, walkthrough, and review.

Inspection is the lowest level of review, appropriate for end products which are small in terms of effort to produce, and are expected to be free of any ambiguous requirements . An inspection usually means that a peer of the author checks the work against its task definition for completeness, against standards for conformance and, as appropriate, for accuracy.

Walkthroughs are conducted at an intermediate level of formality. They are the most appropriate review technique for end products which are medium in terms of effort to produce and relatively free from the possibility of ambiguity in requirements. The author supplies copies of the material to reviewers, who must have some time to familiarise themselves with the material before the walkthrough.

The author leads the meeting and 'walks through' the end product with the reviewers—the object being to ensure that the whole end product is addressed at a reasonable level. The reviewers check the work against its task definition for completeness, against standards for conformance and, as appropriate, for accuracy.

Reviews are formal and are the most appropriate technique for end products which are at a high level of abstraction or cover a wide area and are open to the possibility of ambiguity in requirements. Reviews consist of two stages. The first stage is a paper review to remove obvious faults and ambiguities. The second stage is the formal review meeting. The meeting is controlled by a moderator, who agrees the venue and time with all participants and ensures that all documents for review are distributed in good time.

Reviewers are expected to be properly prepared, which involves checking that the material:

- addresses correctly and completely all requirements in its precursor;
- does not introduce new requirements/facilities other than those necessary to satisfy its precursor;
- is unambiguous and concise;
- contains sufficient detail (but no more) too allow its successor to be produced to the same criteria;
- is internally consistent;
- complies with standards.

Within the review session the moderator has complete control. All other members are equal and 'parliamentary privilege' applies so that people can speak freely, which is essential if the review process is to be fully effective. Reviews are intensive and disciplined and should not exceed two hours.

System deficiencies and corrective actions

Corrective actions recorded at QA audits and reviews relate to errors and deficiencies. In many cases, particularly with reviews, these are specific items which can be corrected locally. Some of the deficiencies, however, are attributable to errors or omissions in the quality system. One activity within the quality system is to capture this information along with other requests for changes to standards and see these changes, if required, are implemented.

Management review

Periodic reviews of the quality system are the key to its continued relevance and value. They are also a mandatory requirement to satisfy ISO9000. The main characteristics of such reviews are:

- They consider all aspects of the quality systems in operation (e.g. do the end products satisfy demand and to what extent does the quality system help?).

- they result in specific improvement actions generally (but not exclusively) resulting in changes to both the system and the standards.

Standards programme

Projects and activities have lifecycles which differ from those of standards. Standards, either general or local, in a particular area may not exist in a satisfactory form at the time projects commence. They may also change during the life of a project. A list of most current major software standards will be found in *Engineering Software Quality*.

In order to prevent problems it is recommended that projects produce quality plans which will, among other things, define procedures where suitable standards are not available, and define the standards and versions applicable.

The need for standards has been recognised for many years. Some of the earliest standards were the cubit, inch and metre. Within the software industry the need was recognised and led to the production of many standards.

Standards are, or at least should be, living, relevant documents, that reflect best current practice. To achieve this within the quality system there needs to be an on-going programme of standards production, review and improvement. The following points are taken from a good standards policy and give a good indication of what is required:

- The standards programme will be based on taking advantage of the best existing practices in cases where these are documented or otherwise well understood and communicated.

- Local standards must be, and be seen to be, produced, reviewed and agreed by practitioners. This will help with users buying in to them.

- Authorisation must be appropriate for the standard, ie standards must be perceived as having the support of a relevant authority.

- Distribution must match the need, so that everyone who needs to use a standard can do so easily and with minimum effort or risk of using the wrong version.

- Procedures for making changes to standards must be readily accessible, easy to use, and users must see that changes they require are evaluated properly and incorporated when appropriate.

- Documents that have not changed should be reviewed for their relevance on a regular basis.

- There should be a formal, controlled mechanism whereby urgent changes can be communicated and implemented rapidly. Also whereby such changes can be incorporated into the formal system in a more relaxed timescale.

- All documents which describe the department's policy, procedures, or standards must state clearly their purpose and scope in a way which is obvious to the reader. They should be seen to help.

We have described the process of managing a quality system—now for some of the known pitfalls. In practice, a QMS provides a firm basis for process improvement—but no more. It will not help solve long-standing problems but will allow people to assess where they are starting from. But first, the QMS has to be successfully installed and (more importantly) embedded as a part of 'the way we do things here'.

A1.4   THE COMMON PITFALLS OF QUALITY

Many QMS implementations fail. The definition of failure is that the system is not leading to improvement in quality. The usual reason for failures as stated earlier are not technical but people related and can be listed as:

- No demonstrated management commitment.

- No user buy-in.

- Wrong people in the quality team.

- QMS too big and bureaucratic.

- Poor communication.

- No perceived added value.

- Complacence and fear of change.

- Lack of appropriate training.

    Each of these will now be expanded.

No demonstrated management commitment

This is usually quoted as no senior management commitment. This hides a major problem because, usually, senior management *are* committed. They see a need, as do the staff at the coal face, and want to work in a quality way.

    The real problem is, more often, the middle management who do not have the time to change existing practice and see the QMS as being irrelevant to their day-to-day problems.

Commitment to quality has to be demonstrated not just by commitment of resources but also by action. Demonstration of this commitment will help the rest to buy in to the QMS.

No user buy-in

If a QMS is to succeed it must show a benefit for all the users. This benefit will depend upon the user viewpoint. The man or woman hacking the code will see benefits in doing it in a controlled manner providing there is not too much bureaucracy. The senior management will appreciate the control and description of the work. The advantages to middle management will be a combination of these two but will require input and participation.

One of the best ways of ensuring buy-in is to get the user to produce some part of the system or at least be involved in the review. The key to getting user buy-in is to look for small victories to begin with. These must show a quick return to the users, the object being to leave them with a warm feeling about quality.

Wrong people in the quality team

From the previous chapter, you will see that the installation and maintenance of a QMS will require it to be actively pushed and sold. To succeed you need to be a quality zealot. If you want an easy life, stay out of the quality team.

QMS too bureaucratic

The size of documentation required to run a quality management system can vary from one thin volume to a couple of yards on a shelf. As the system evolves it usually shrinks in size. The question to be answered is: will what we document improve the quality of our product or service? If not, why write it?

In practice, the amount of time spent on administration is cited as the main failing with having a QMS. If this extra administration is not effective, problems ensue—see below.

Poor communication

Most major problems within projects can be attributed to a failure of communications at some stage. The QMS will insist that you will document your contract review and other agreements both with customers and suppliers. This will help to reduce any misunderstandings. Internal communications are also a problem. If the QMS is seen to help and not hinder communications, it will help sell the system.

No perceived added value

If the QMS is not seen to help the user or add value to the process, it will not be used. All the staff from the senior managers to the workers at the coal face will find reason for not using the system.

This can be a problem both when installing a QMS and when the system has been running for several years. In the early stages the formality and extra documentation are seen as an unnecessary overhead. The key here is to sell the system and keep it simple. Always ensure the documentation is really needed and is seen to add value to the process.

Once the system has been running and is accepted as part of the normal work, if is not seen to change to meet the customers' perceived requirements, then the question of added value will again occur. The system must be seen as living and changing to meet the evolving requirements of the user.

Complacency

Complacency and the other side of the coin, fear of change, can be problems for the installation and implementation of the QMS. The complacency is usually manifested by statements such as 'we are a quality organisation why do we need a QMS?' or 'we have always done it this way and no one has complained.' The same statements are used to mask fear of change. The only way to overcome both of these problems is by showing areas that can be improved and by getting buy-in to these improvements. If a new procedure is required, get the person it most affects to write it or at least review it.

Lack of appropriate training

One of the major problems with quality is training. One of the American gurus stated, to get the quality message across, tell them, tell them again and again and keep on telling them. This is a simplistic view but the message is correct. You need to invest in training and this investment must be ongoing. This training is the driver for constant improvement.

A1.5   A D-I-Y GUIDE TO INSTALLING A QMS

To help avoid some of the above problems (and a few of the other more avoidable pitfalls) we end this appendix with a checklist for the installation of a QMS. A word of warning: use this (and any other checklist for that matter) as an aide memoire, not a bible.

1. Secure senior management commitment:
   - Don't start until you have it.

2. Appoint someone to project manage the implementation:
   - Train them.

3. Establish the current state of affairs in the company:
   - Conduct a survey.
   - Raise awareness.
   - Obtain support.

4. Establish the QMS objectives:
   - Obtain a clear idea of what you want them to do—essential in order to measure achievement.

5. Establish organisation and responsibility structure:
   - Probably exists already but needs formalising.
   - Establish job descriptions.
   - Use common format and establish simple review procedure.

6. Agree with line managers the critical functions and activities which need to be procedurally controlled:
   - Draw flow charts of activities.
   - Identify interfaces and critical quality-affecting processes.

7. Develop the quality manual:
   - Designed to ISO9000 standard.
   - Keep it short and simple; easy to update and in plain English relevant to *your* business.

8. Establish buy-in:
   - Arrange awareness sessions little and often is better than one 'sheep dip'.

9. Prepare procedure/work instructions:
   - Adopt simple standard format.
   - Get the users to write and own them.

- The writer is the reviewer.

- Keep them short and simple.

- Use diagrams and flowcharts.

- Remember the skills of your people—don't write unnecessary instructions, only those that add value to the process.

10. Implement the system:

- Launch, train people in the system and begin to keep records.

- Establish regular reviews during the early phases to improve untested procedures.

- Appoint and train the auditors.

- Commence the audit programme.

A1.6   HEALTHCHECK SURVEY CHECKLISTS

1. Project management

1. Are the project objectives and customer constraints well defined and documented?

2. Does the customer formally approve the project?

3. Are a number of independent estimation techniques (e.g. analogy, algorithmic cost model, checklists) used, and the results compared and analysed to come up with an overall effort estimate? Are historical data used to support any of the estimation techniques?

4. Are the estimation process and results documented along with the assumptions and risks that have a bearing on the estimate, and the estimate reviewed with higher management and the customer?

5. Is there any documented result of an attempt to identify potential project risks? Are the risks assessed and prioritised in terms of their likelihood of occurrence and their potential impact on the project?

6. Are as many viewpoints as possible (not just the project team) involved in the risk assessment process?

7. Is there a hierarchical set of plans (or at least high-level and detailed plans) identifying roles and responsibilities, end products, lifecycle stages, etc? Are individuals named against activities for firm plans?

8. Is there a risk management plan (or equivalent) indicating how high priority risks will be resolved and stating how risks will be monitored?

9. Are estimation techniques re-applied regularly to predict the latest forecast project completion?

10. Is there regular reporting both internally to the project and between the project manager and customer?

11. Are the project management and control procedures fully documented, and well integrated with the development lifecycle?

12. Are projects formally closed? (Are all end products complete? Does the customer sign off the project? Are staff working on the project notified that it is complete? Is an end-of-project report written?)

2. Requirements capture and analysis

1. Is one single authority (within the customer organisation) identified who has the final decision in all aspects of the requirements, and is that person appropriately involved in the RCA process and prepared to make the necessary commitments to tasks and to decisions? (In the case of large projects, is a *structure* of customer representatives and user groups *defined* with authority to make specific decisions?)

2. Is the business need for the system or enhancement being specified clear to the analysis team: for example, is the business case available to them?

3. Does the analysis team have the following mix of expertise: experience of the application area ; experience of the RCA approach being used; experience of the development of software systems within the application area? In addition, do members of the team have the interpersonal skills necessary to work with a wide range of customers and users?

4. Are attempts made to educate customers: firstly, in the importance of having a good specification; secondly, in the potential and limitations of computer solutions?

5. Does the analysis team identify and involve all relevant stakeholders and their viewpoints in the RCA process?

6. Does the analysis team pay as much attention to job and business design as it does to computer systems, and are the resultant system qualities (for example safety, security, performance, usability, portability) and learning requirements fully expressed?

7. Is the analysis team careful to determine relative priorities of requirements (where appropriate) and are the reasons for the priorities recorded?

8. Does the analysis team encourage and control frequent communication between themselves and the stakeholders in order to ensure that it shares a common vision with the stakeholders of how the proposed system is expected to be used? (This could be done by considering scenarios of system usage, building prototypes of part of the system, walking through models of the system.)

9. Does the analysis team consider *all* the relevant users of the SOR when they prepare it? Users of the SOR can include designers (for developing the system), testers (for writing test specifications), customers (for validation and agreement), other stakeholders (for validation), technical authors (for preparation of user documentation), technical management (for analysis of the risk of the proposed development), marketing (for inclusion of the proposed system in marketing strategies).

10. Does the analysis team operate a formal change control scheme on the requirements which includes: prioritisation of proposed changes; authorisation of changes; issue control of the SOR.

11. Are computer support tools used to maintain the requirements and to check for consistency?

Note: definition of terms used in the RCA checklist:

Analysis team. The team of people who undertake the RCA exercise. Depending on circumstances, it may include customers, users, strategists, developers, dedicated analysts.

Customer. The person who is responsible for ensuring the business and strategic requirements for the proposed system (or enhancement) are correct. This may be the person who authorises the budget for the system.

SOR. Statement of Requirements. The output from the specification activity in the RCA process. Covers user requirements rather than system specification.

Stakeholder. People, organisations and existing systems that are affected by or which influence the proposed system development or enhancement. Will include the customer and users. Note that stakeholders can be interested in qualities of the proposed system (such as safety, security, data standards, performance) as well as functions.

User. Either people who will use the proposed system (or enhancement) or who are existing users of current systems.

3. Verification, validation and testing

1. Are there procedures or work instructions within the unit defining the VV&T methods and practices to be used?

2. Is there a lifecycle covering development and VV&T with clearly defined stages and end-products?

3. Is a VV&T plan or top level strategy produced for every project, describing the overall VV&T approach, roles and responsibilities, schedule of activities, objectives for VV&T, methods, techniques and tools to be used?

4. Are test plans produced covering each testing phase, i.e. acceptance, system, integration and unit testing?

5. Are V&V techniques such as reviews, inspections, walkthroughs used to check specification, design and test documents for completeness, correctness and consistency?

6. Is the requirements specification analysed for testability?

7. Is the test process documented, i.e. are test specifications, test designs, test cases and test reports produced?

8. Do the people working on VV&T within the unit have the necessary experience and training in the skills required?

9. Are VV&T activities carried out by people who are independent from developers?

10. Are tools used to automate testing where possible?

11. Are metrics on defect data gathered and analysed to provide feedback to management to enable improvements to be made?

4. Metrication

1. Does the unit monitor planned versus actual cost?

2. Does the unit monitor planned versus actual schedule?

3. Does the unit use a documented procedure or tool to estimate cost and schedule? Does this involve the comparison of estimates reached by different methods? (Not necessarily an arithmetic model. Comparing estimates reached by, eg., functionality versus task allocation is fine.)

4. Does the unit record and use the number of faults found at testing and post-release?

5. Is the fault data which is collected analysed to determine root causes?

6. Does the unit monitor the set of modules during development (or maintenance) to spot unusual (and therefore potentially problematic) modules?

7. Does the unit assess customer satisfaction?

8. Are end-project reviews carried out, and data on cost and timescales recorded?

9. Does the unit keep any other metrics?

5. Design

1. Are the critical parts of the project given special attention?

2. Are design walkthroughs and reviews held, which include reviewers from outside the design team?

3. Are standards in place to define the design process for any given project?

4. Does the design approach chosen fit any specific acceptance criteria laid down for the project as a whole?

5. Has previous experience of the team been taken into account in the choice of design method for the project, and if not, has training been planned?

6. Has the category and size of system being designed been acknowledged in the choice of the design approach?

7. If the project requirements change frequently, has some provision been made for coping with this in the design approach?

8. If the customer's involvement in the design process is important, has provision for this been made in the design approach?

9. Is it straightforward to produce and update project documentation?

10. Have performance and reliability requirements been taken into account in the design approach?

11. Are the external interfaces of the system known, and are these and the internal interfaces between project elements reviewed?

12. Do the designers know how and to what extent their design options are constrained by existing hardware and software?

6. Configuration management

1. Do you use CM tools?

2. Is a documented Naming Convention used?

3. Do you have a system for managing and controlling problems?

4. Does the project have a CM plan?

5. Are all procedures defined in the CM plan being followed?

6. Are your team members aware of their documented CM roles and responsibilities?

7. Is information recorded and reported on the status of project items (e.g. software, documentation and change requests)?

8. Is access to the repository restricted to those who need it?

9. Is authorisation required before a change can be made?

10. Do you take baseline records at key points within a project?

11. Are rigorous CM controls exercised over all components, including those externally supplied?

12. Is your CM system audited at least every six months?

7. Performance engineering

1. Do you assess the size (and cost) of the target hardware platform for your system (e.g. CPU, disks, memory)?

2. Do you have a clear idea of all sources and volumes of workload on your system, when operational?

3. Is there a full quantitative specification of the performance and workload requirements for your system, e.g. in terms of user-perceived response time and transaction rate?

4. During system design, do you identify potential user loading and its impact on performance?

5. Do you produce a system model in order to predict performance characteristics?

6. Do you plan, specify and document performance tests?

7. Do you have the means to carry out repeatable testing under operational load conditions?

8. Have you a clear idea of your system's behaviour when subjected to sustained overload?

9. Do the customer acceptance criteria include demonstrations of adequate performance and workload throughput?

10. Are performance and workload statistics gathering facilities built into the applications?

11. Do post-release support plans include performance support, for example system tuning, performance reporting, performance troubleshooting?

12. Is an operational hardware capacity plan drawn up?

8. Maintenance and release

1. Does the software system have a release schedule, defining the changes to be incorporated and the date of release?

2. Is the customers' documentation updated with each release? This includes details of changes to functionality, release notes, and details of the problems fixed.

3. Are there formal procedures for building new releases of software to ensure that correct components/modules are incorporated?

4. Are there formal procedures for distributing the newly built and tested software? Confidence testing, packaging, delivery, and customer's acceptance testing should be considered here, i.e. getting the right product to the customer in good condition, and ensuring that it works on the customers' premises.

5. Is there a formal process for maintenance, from problem reporting to system release?

6. Does the maintenance team have a high level of experience in maintenance techniques? (These include effective control of change requests and problem handling, reliable configuration management, and code analysis).

7. Does the maintenance team have modern code comprehension tools which allow the structure of software to be examined and modified, and do they know how to use these tools properly? (Such tools should allow the maintainers to analyse the complexity of code, identifying redundancy, duplication and over-complex areas.)

8. Is there a system for maintaining documentation as part of the maintenance process? Is this always enforced (or generated automatically, e.g. by CASE tools)?

9. Are the consequences of proposed changes fully evaluated, e.g. ripple effects, altered functionality?

10. Is there a clearly defined procedure for updating system tests when the functionality of the code has changed due to a change request?

11. Does the maintenance team have easy access to the machines on which the software runs, or identical copies?

12. Are there formal, signed agreements for the support work?

REFERENCES

The following are general rather than specific references to quality management systems and their implementation:

International Standard ISO 9000-3 Quality Management and Quality Assurance Standards, part 3. Reference number ISO9000-3:1991(e)
Rigby P J, Stoddart A G and Norris M T (1990) *BT Engineering Journal* **8** 244
Deming's 14 Points For Management The British Deming Association, 2 Castle Street, Salisbury, Wiltshire SP11BB, UK
Smith D J and Wood K B (1989) *Engineering Software Quality* Elsevier

Appendix 2

Useful Product Measures and How to Get Them

> *When you can measure what you are speaking about and*
> *express it in numbers, you know something about it.*
> *When you cannot measure it, when you cannot express it in*
> *numbers, your knowledge is a meagre and unsatisfactory kind*
>
> Lord Kelvin

> *An approximate answer to the right question is better than a*
> *precise answer to the wrong one*
>
> Anon

> *Metrics is crap*
>
> E Dijkstra

> *What gets measured gets done*
>
> Anon

The four quotes used above indicate the range of views on measurement. Software measurement may be a far from exact science but sensible indicators of product quality can be derived. This appendix is intended to provide a reference for establishing a workable and useful product measurement system within both a software development and procurement context. It contains definitions of a selection of practical software product metrics[1] and some guidelines for their interpretation.

---

[1] To avoid confusion it should be explained that the term 'metric' is used here only to denote a rigorous description of a particular measurement procedure. The terms 'measure' and 'measurement' are used to refer to the action of measuring, or to a value resulting from such an action. 'Measure' is also used as a synonym for 'metric'.

The introductory section looks at the different types of software measurements and the general procedures for collecting data. We then explain how the end product measures collected can be combined to provide 'quality indicators' (measures which directly reflect some aspect of the quality of a product). We also give an indication of which metrics may be of special interest to particular individuals, e.g. project managers, developers, maintainers or customers, but first a little background.

A2.1   UNDERSTANDING SOFTWARE MEASUREMENT

It is an important principle that in order to understand something you first should attempt to categorise it, in terms of something which you already understand. There are a number of ways of putting software measures into categories in order to understand them better. In line with the main text of this book, two categories which appear amenable to objective measurement are those of software product and process. An example of a product would be a piece of code, a measure of which would be the number of lines of code. An example of a process would be a software lifecycle with the process measure being that of its duration in time.

However, this apparently simple approach can be seen to be less useful when it is realised that product measures are often interpreted as telling you something about the process, and vice versa. For example, the statement 'It is a good software development process. I know this because all of the products we produced using it were successful' assumes a relationship that may or may not be true. A similar example, 'I know it is a reliable system because we have only had to spend two days doing the maintenance on it during the whole of the last year' is equally ill-founded.

The fact is that software products and processes are so linked together that it is the *use* to which measurements are put that determines whether they are product or process measures, rather than the measures themselves. Most of the measures included in this document are intended to be used as product measurements in spite of the fact that many of them can also be used as process measures.

From here, further categorisation is possible. Two basic types of end-product measurements can be defined:

- Internal measures based on a white box view of the software representation itself (i.e. static measures). Well known examples of these include McCabe's control flow metric [McC76] and Henry and Kafura's information flow metric [HK81].

- External measures based on a black box view of the end product (i.e. the '...ilities'). Again, these can be further decomposed, for example, into:

  - Dynamic measures, i.e. measures with an operational time element, related to the software system (or components of it) in operation. A good example of this is to equate reliability to the failure rate of the software in operation. Other dynamic attributes, such as availability and integrity, can be defined similarly.

- Activity measures, i.e. measures, typically with an effort element, of the activities of people working with the software. For instance, we could relate maintainability to the effort expended by maintainers in repairing faults or usability to the effort expended by users in learning to operate 90% of the system features.

The above provides no more than a broad scope for how the measures of the software product can be categorised. The key point that should be borne in mind throughout, though, is that you need to have a clear idea of the goal of using a particular measure (or set of measures). Only then can you ask the right questions that imply the relevant measures [Ham85]. The remainder of this appendix covers the planning and interpretation of a measurement programme, once the goal is fixed.

A2.2   PLANNING A METRICS PROGRAMME

Given the caveats above, there a number of readily applicable and useful quality metrics. Many of these have been tested on real data, collected at many software development sites . Before any of these metrics can be applied, though, a knowledge of the data collection and analysis processes must be acquired. The following is a brief description of some of these processes. A considerable amount of the practical detail on the installation of a company-wide metrics programme can be found in [GC92].

1. Identifying which data to collect

This is a very important factor in ensuring that the data is collected correctly and that the metrics are useful to, for instance, the development and maintenance teams. In order to identify which data should be collected, the purpose of the data collection should be known, the cost of collecting the data should be estimated (and sufficient resources made available) and the development team should understand the benefits to be gained from collecting this data.

2. Defining the data to be collected

Once the data to be collected has been identified, these definitions will need to be rewritten to take account of the standards, terminology and measurement units used within the particular project. These definitions must be understood by all members of the project.

3. Establishing data collection methods, controls and procedures

These must be defined in order to ensure that the data is collected in a systematic way, that it is validated (i.e. it is complete and consistent), that all necessary training has been arranged, that responsibilities have been assigned, that (where possible) tools for data collection have been provided and that feedback mechanisms for data analysis results have been arranged.

4. Planning for data storage and analysis

These constituents of a metrics programme are often neglected during the planning stage, with consideration being put off until later. As a result it is only after a lack of resources and facilities becomes apparent, during and after the data collection activity itself, that they are remembered. In order to make full use of the data collected, these components of metrics programmes must be planned and resourced before the start of the data collection itself.

5. Providing tool support

A wide range of tools for data collection, analysis and storage are currently available (and more tools are being developed all the time). An entirely paper-based metrics data collection exercise is unlikely to be a viable proposition—some tool support is essential in practice [KNP93].

A2.3   PRODUCING RELEVANT DATA

It is often not possible to collect software measurements which can *directly* measure aspects of quality or which can be used to predict those aspects. Measures which have these abilities themselves might be referred to as true 'figures of merit'. One example of this would be the measure 'Mean time to failure' in the case of software reliability.

In most cases, though, the measures which are collected have to be processed (as a part of a data analysis exercise) before they can be used as quality indicators [BS84]. Two processing techniques which may be used for this are briefly explained below.

Combining end product measures

It is assumed here that the system being measured is defined in terms of modules, sub-modules and datafiles/stores. In order to compare different measures of these, it is important to ensure that the measures being combined to give the overall picture have been applied to the same level of component (i.e. system, module or sub-module).

Where tools have been used, the level of component to be measured is fixed. Therefore, when comparing measures from different levels of component, it will be necessary to combine the lower level measures in some way, first, so as to produce compatible measures.

This can be achieved by summing the measures for the sub-modules (or modules) to give an overall measure for the module (or system) or calculating the mean or median.

Composite metrics

Another way in which measures may need to be combined is when a composite measurement is required. The most familiar example of this is probably programmer productivity, a measure which involves taking separate measurements of different objects (namely people and time and lines of code) and then combining them into one figure such as 'number of lines of code per personday'.

This serves to emphasise the difference between some measures which are collected directly and which may be combined to provide composite measures (this might be called raw measurement data), and other measures which have been constructed from this raw measurement data (which could be called processed measurement data). Most established metrics fall into the category of raw measurement data, so that in some cases it may not be entirely obvious why the data should be collected. Only when the final composite measures, to which they will contribute, are determined does the light dawn.

A2.4   SELECTING METRICS

It is not advised that a project collect every known measure—this would achieve very little and probably take forever. A suitable subset of measures should be selected for the job in hand. Which measures are selected will depend on several factors, namely:

- the purpose for which the data is being collected;
- the type of project; the usefulness of the measures;
- the maturity of the organisation or environment.

This section is intended to assist in selecting which of the proposed measures should be included in a particular metrics programme.

Viewpoints and attributes

The ultimate aim of a measurement programme is to improve quality. But quality, on its own, is too general a concept to be useful, so it is commonly broken down into a set of attributes. These attributes should be defined and chosen on the basis of being non-overlapping (in so far as is possible) and as being relevant to specific viewpoints. Thus, for example a set of '-ility' attributes (maintainability, testability, and enhancability) may be taken as key drivers for the selection of product measures.

Progressive stages in measurement

The selection of metrics is also likely to be affected by the relative maturity of the organisation or environment into which they are going to be introduced. For this reason it is suggested that four progressive stages of quality measurement should be considered and a choice made concerning the target level of entry.

The *first stage* might be called the *absolute minimum stage*; that is to say, a bare minimum of metrics in order to begin to create a measurement culture within the organisation, and to get a handle on some product characteristics and quality issues. Their initial introduction is in practice often carried out on a fairly ad hoc basis with no clear programme, and does not involve substantial investment being made. Indeed in some organisations measurement data is being collected in this way but is not recognised as being metrics as such.

The *second stage* (which might be called the *process or project improvement approach*) would involve a substantial investment in collecting measurement data with the goal of overall process or individual project improvement within a particular software development environment. This would only indirectly be aimed at the production of better quality products as opposed to better quality processes.

This stage can also involve attempting to increase efficiency within projects, and to detect 'hot spots' in the development process which require special attention. Another goal of this approach might be to spot potential problems in advance, so that they can be sorted out before they occur.

A *third stage* (which might be called the *product quality assessment approach*), would involve a determined exercise in measuring specific product quality attributes at delivery or release time for assessment purposes. This would allow, for instance, the establishment of a feedback link to the specification established at the requirements capture stage, in order to check if targets were being met.

In addition, apart from the direct benefits of establishing such a feedback loop, there is the added prospect of building up a database of historical information on product quality levels. This in the long term could be used to monitor the effects on product quality levels of the introduction of new methods and working practices within an organisation. Potentially this could lead to the ability to tailor development processes for the production of specific product characteristics, as well as the overall improvement of processes.

At the *fourth stage*, attempts are being made to predict product quality in advance of the implementation stage. This is still an experimental procedure (in spite of the claims of certain static analysis tool vendors) but its potential benefits are many. They include making changes to designs early on in the lifecycle so as to improve future products quality, as well as eventually being able to design particular quality attributes into the software.

There are many organisations at the first or second stages, but scarcely any which have progressed to the third stage. There is often a temptation to try to jump ahead of stage three and use tools which attempt to predict potential product quality problems, even though there are no means of actually measuring the product's quality. This is a recipe for self-delusion, since in this case there is no way of proving if quality is improving or getting worse as a result of using the tools. It is better to walk before you attempt to run, if you want to avoid falling over!

By way of example, the following four metrics could be associated with the four stages:

Stage 1 - Lines of code for each module.
Stage 2 - Lifecycle stage of origin for each fault.
Stage 3 - Effort expended for each fault-fix.
Stage 4 - Measures of control flow complexity.

A2.5   QUALITY METRICS DEFINITIONS

This section defines a few of the more useful software metrics which can be used for data collection with existing technology. However, in a real data collection exercise it is likely that only a subset of the available metrics would be selected for use. Apart from the factors affecting this selection which have been mentioned already, practical concerns such as the availability of tools, pre-existing data collection procedures allowing the reuse of data, and the need to restrict costs, are all likely to have some influence.

The quality metrics described below are grouped according to the different types of data to be collected. The types or categories do not refer to the use to which the measurement data will be put, but to the objects being measured in each case. Thus the end product measures are all measures of the code, and the environmental measures are measures of the environment within which the software is being developed.

The types include development data (i.e. project data), measures of the final product, fault and failure related data, and environmental data.

Development effort

Number of person days of effort expended for each distinct stage of the development lifecycle of the project . The inclusion or exclusion of support resources (including management overheads) should be registered along with this data. In addition, various, non-numeric characteristics of the project (such as languages used, hardware employed, clerical support availability, use of CASE tools, or application of structured programming methods) should be recorded. This is particularly important if this data is to be used for future cost estimation.

Configuration management metrics

This set of measures relates to number of changes to a particular file or set of files as it goes through development. They offer an indication of the reliability of modules, etc, as well as giving some feel for testability and maintainability. For each module, the main measures are

- The interval. How long the item is taken out of the master file before an updated version is replaced.

- The total number of configuration items, both in the master file and being worked on.

- The number of replacements per unit time.

- The total number of differences or altered lines between removal and replacement.

The way in which these can be fitted together to provide effective tracking is illustrated in the project recovery chapter (7) of this book.

Failure and fault metrics

This set of metrics is closely related to the configuration management set. In this instance, the action taken on the item is added. For example, if a particular module is removed for repair, the root cause of the problem with the module would be recorded. Thus, the above list would be supplemented with category of fault, cause of fault, how serious, etc. The application of fault metrics is illustrated in the main text.

End product metrics

This is easily the biggest (and probably most difficult to interpret) set of measures. Rather than go through all the code/design measures that are available, a few of the more useful ones are detailed below. Included are some guidelines on what they mean and when they should start the alarm bells ringing [IS88].

A more comprehensive list of end-product metrics is given (in less detail) at the end of this appendix.

A2.6   EXAMPLE PRODUCT MEASURES

For each of the five metrics in this section, we give a brief definition, and example (if appropriate) and some observation on practical application.

(1) McCabe cyclomatic complexity (MCC)

Definition. This is a measure of the structural decision complexity of a basic component, and as such it has become very well known. It basically counts the number of decision alternatives in a program. A high value correlates with complexity and hence increased test and maintenance effort.

The McCabe metric is defined as = #edges − #nodes +2.

Example
```
if ..{}            switch .. { case a: {}
else if ..{}            case b: {}
else if .. {}           case c: {}
else......                default: {}
```

Both have a McCabe value of 4.

Metric value ranges and warning limits
Metric values range from 0 to 100, although in C programs values larger than 30 are very rare.
Warning limit = 10. Critical limit = 15.

(2) Maximum depth of nesting (DEP)

Definition. This measures the maximum depth of nesting of a flowgraph. A nesting node in a flowgraph is a decision point/statement in a basic component.

High metric values imply that the decision logic is complex. Therefore the error-proneness of components with a high depth of nesting is high. One possible exception can be found if a designer applies the following programming style:

```
if a then ...
else if ............
else ............
```

In some cases the usage of a CASE statement could be more appropriate in the example above.

Example

```
function x ()
{
    while not stop {
      if a {...}
      }
}
```

A component with an if-statement nested into a while-loop has a nesting value of 2.

Metric value ranges and warning limits
Metrics values can range from 0 to 50. Values larger than 9 are very rare.
Warning limit = 4. Critical limit = 7.

(3) Number of nodes (NN)

Definition. This is a pure size metric. It counts the number of 'statements' in a basic component, and as such it is a very good approximation of the well known metric LOC (lines of code).

Observation studies have shown a reasonably high correlation between error-proneness, readability and maintainability. A good coding strategy is to always keep your basic components acceptably small. Limits for the number of nodes can serve as an early warning to see if the size of code is growing out of hand. In that case a basic component could be split up into smaller separate parts.

Metric value ranges and warning limits
Values can range from 0 to 1000, but values larger than 100 should not occur, especially in structured programming languages.
Warning limit = 20. Critical limit = 40.

(4) Number of calls (NC)

Definition. This counts the number of function/procedure calls in a basic component. It is therefore an information flow metric. The more function calls, the larger the dependency on other parts of a program (high coupling). In order to understand or modify the functionality of this basic component one has to know much about the functionality of other basic components. A high value correlates with difficulty of modifying the behaviour of the basic components.

Metric value ranges and warning limits
Values normally range from 0 to 50. Values larger than 20 are seldom seen.
Warning limit = 8. Critical limit = 15.

(5) Static path count (NUM)

Definition. This counts all possible paths from the start-node to the end-node of a basic component, under the assumption that any loop can either be executed zero or one time. The influence of unconditional control transfers is completely ignored.

The metric is based upon summing up the possible paths in a nesting, and by multiplying the possible paths of sequenced flowgraphs (these all yield unique paths).

This measure can be used to set an upper bound on the possible distinct paths through a basic component. If it is high, then it will be hard to guarantee full path-testing coverage, since there are so many possibilities. Very high values should especially be avoided in high reliability environments.

Example

```
        if (a = = b) { if c! = d {. . .}
                } else {....}
        else

for (....) {....}

        if (e = =f) {....}
        else {....}
```

The example program segment above has a static path value of 12.

Metric value ranges and warning limits
Warning limit = 100. Critical limit = 500

A2.7   IS THERE A 'BEST' METRIC?

Are there any true short cuts to measuring the software product? Code metrics which can predict quality appear to offer a beguiling alternative to the apparently expensive options of establishing process measurement systems within organisations. If such 'best metrics' exist then merely by checking software against them, future quality improvements could be assured.

In reality, if such product metrics are ever going to emerge, it will have to be after the routine measurement of actual system product quality has been well established, as it is hardly possible to accurately predict something which is not being measured in the first place.

Accordingly the answer to the question must depend upon what you want to use the metric for in the first place. A number of basic uses of metrics are listed below (Table A2.1) in table format, along with the names of suggested metrics for each use. These tables are based upon a number of observation trials which sought to correlate product measure with actual performance. To simplify the presentation of the tables, the individual metrics which appear in the lists are referred to by identifying codes according to the following schema:

Thousands of lines of non-comment source code = KLN
Thousands of lines of variable declaration code = KLV
Thousands of lines of comment code = KLC
The 'McCabe cyclomatic complexity' metric = MCC
The 'maximum depth of nesting' metric = DEP
The 'product VINAP' metric = VIN
The 'Prather' metric = PRA
The 'number of paths' metric = NUM
The 'branch testing' metric = BRT
The 'number of simple paths' metric = SIM
The 'henry and kafura' metric = HK
KLV/KLN-KLV as a measure of data orientation = DO
KLC/KLN as a measure of communicativeness = CO

In the case of metrics which apply to functions as opposed to modules, the values were combined in different ways in order to represent the parent modules. Suffixes are added to the metrics' codes in order to indicate if they are combined by summing (SU), averaging (ME), a weighted mean (WM), or taking a density estimate (DE).

As indicated, some of the metrics have been found across a number of trials to be better than others, but whether such recommendations are generally applicable can only be discovered through more trials across a range of application and business areas [KP87].

The final message in this section is that the best measures are those which draw on local experience. For instance, part of the authors' local guidelines read as follows:

(a) For coding and testing of finite state machine (FSM) based modules, allow 0.6 days per separate action called by the state machine. Allow an average of 50 lines of code per action.

(b) Note that these are only averages and that the days per action figure can range from 0.4 to 0.9 depending on the complexity of the action. Likewise, the lines per action can range from 35 to 75.

(c) For the full development lifecycle of an FSM module ie. requirements, design code and module test, allow 1.2 days per action, with a range of 0.9 to 1.6.

The percentages of the total effort allocated to the main categories of activity in the project are as follows:

Management   11%
Design documentation, (including internal requirements
   specifications)   18%

Metric family >	Size metrics			Control flow metrics										Inf flow
Recommended metrics > / Reason for collecting metrics	KLN	KLV(DO)	KLC(CO)	DEPDE	DEPWM	DEPSU	VINDE	VINSU	NUMWM	PRASU	BRTWM	SIMSU	MCCDE	HK
Quality:														
Predicting quality before testing														
1. Module correctness	•				•									
2. Module fault density	•	•		•										•
Predicting future quality at release														
1. Module correctness	•				•			•	•					
2. Module fault density	•	•				•	•			•			•	•
3. Module performance								•			•			
4. Module maintainability	•					•								
5. Module code maintainability	•		•								•			•
Cost:														
Predicting costs at release														
1. Module maintainability	•								•		•			•
2. Module code maintainability	•		•											

KLN   = 000s of lines of non-comment source code
KLV   = 000s of lines of variable declaration
KLC   = 000s of lines of comment code
DEPDE = maximum depth of nesting, density version
DEPWM = maximum depth of nesting, weighted mean version
DEPSU = maximum depth of nesting, sum version
VINDE = the 'Product VINAP' metric, density version

VINSU = the 'Product VINAP' metric, sum version
NUMWM = the 'Number of Paths' metrics, weighted mean version
PRASU = the 'Prather' metric, sum version
BRTWM = the 'Branch Testing' metric, weighted mean version
SIMSU = the 'Number of Simple Paths' metric, sum version
MCCDE = the 'McCabe Cyclomatic Complexity' metric, density version
HK   = Henry Kafura, an information flow measure

(DO) indicates a measure of data orientation
(CO) indicates a measure of communicativeness

Table A2.1   Table of measures (reproduced by permission of British Telecommunications plc)

Test documents (i.e. module, integration and system test specs and
   designs)   15%
Coding and module testing   25%
Sub-system and integration testing
including fault correction and retesting   8%
System testing and rework up to customer acceptance   10%
User guides   3%
Miscellaneous (training, familiarisation, audit follow-up, etc)   10%

Note that the production of the overall requirement specification is not
included in the above figures. It is not expected that all real-time projects
will conform exactly to this pattern, but experience has shown that variations of more than 5 percentage points for the above figures would be
unusual and would need to be justified by some special circumstances.

The figures in this 'formula' draw on the history of similar developments in
which actual times, etc, were recorded and used for the next estimate.

A2.8   COLLECTION OF STATISTICS—A GUIDE FOR PROJECT MANAGERS

Now that we have established a technical base, we can give some usable
guidelines for project managers on how to collect the measure they need and
their customers want. The first point here is that the human dimension to
software engineering should always be borne in mind when figures are
involved. The facts about software systems can become like blurred pho-
tographs of their creators. It is no good looking for crisp lines in such pictures. The effects of the blurring are two-fold, on the one hand the
underlying structures are obscured, and on the other hand a 'work of art'
like uniqueness is introduced into every system that is constructed. As a
result, software metrics contain a lot of 'noise' and the use of statistical analysis for their interpretation cannot be avoided.

Collecting software metrics data is easy enough if tools are used, managing it is time-consuming but not difficult. However, analysing and inter-
preting software metrics data is an exceptionally hard task, and can only be
countenanced with the assistance of statistics. Trials to establish standards,
norms, guidelines, etc involve a lot of statistical analysis, to evaluate the usefulness of different techniques. From the authors' experience, the following
recommendations for software development managers result:

What to use

Most of the analysis routines which are required can be carried out using
Microsoft Excel or a similar spreadsheet. There is little point in buying a

statistical analysis package unless either it has been custom made for metrics data analysis, or else it has the data management facilities which you require in order to access your data in the correct form.

Planning in advance

You must make sure that where possible the objects which you are measuring are the same for each measure. It is difficult to change function measures into module measures, and impossible to do the opposite accurately.

It is worth classifying the measurement objects in different ways, so that measures of objects belonging to different classes can be analysed separately. An example would be a study of metrics applied to all of the modules included in a particular release.

Modules, sub-systems and systems can be measured as unit objects or else as chunks of code. Measures based on the chunk of code model are best for comparisons as opposed to assessments.

Inspecting the data

During the Second World War, it was noticed that some of the Allied bombers suffered much heavier losses than others. There was little obvious reason why this was so and it remained a mystery until some bright spark started to do some tests. He plotted the damage to all bombers returning from raids and noticed that they shared two common features—no bullets or flak either under the pilot's seat or in the tail duct. This correlation immediately solved the problem. The two areas were armoured—and within days this type of bomber was recording the same loss figures as any other. The message is clear: correlating real events clarifies the source of problems.

Scatter plots of one metric against another done at random are only really useful for checking data sets for errors. Outlying values may be the results of mistakes, which checking could eliminate.

Studying the coefficient of variation (CV) of different metrics is useful. Metrics with higher CVs are likely to be more useful for discriminating between different modules, and thus more effective pointers to module quality.

Spotting problems

In general it is enough to study the top 10 or 15% of values in any metrics data set, as higher values nearly always mean worse quality. If a module falls in the top range of more than one metric then it is likely to be a potential troublemaker.

Assessing quality

Measures which assess entire systems consisting of numbers of modules, should be presented in various forms. In particular presenting the mean and standard deviation of the module measures as a system measure is recommended as a means of detecting the presence of 'rogue' modules in a system.

If adequate fault data is not available it may be possible to derive a 'nearly as useful' equivalent measure from a configuration management tool. One such measure is: the number of cycles whereby each module was removed and replaced in the library. Three easily derivable measures for assessing the quality of maintenance processes are,

- Average delay between when fault and fix rates hit peaks and troughs.
- Average time to deliver a fault fix.
- Average time to fix a fault.

These can be applied to different classes of fault reports.

Predicting and improving quality

The lines of code metric appears to be the major contributor to or indicator of the presence of faults in software code. A logical conclusion from this is that using 'higher level' programming languages which require fewer lines to express a particular idea should reduce the overall number of faults in systems.

Metrics-based checking rules may lead to improvements in software quality. Metric value cut-offs based upon observed mean, median, or upper quartile values of metrics of known significance, would be a convenient way of implementing this. Such values would have to be based on a large sample of projects before they could be relied upon. Some indicative values were given earlier in this appendix.

Techniques such as correlation analysis or multiple regression analysis are not recommended for use by busy managers, unless they are incorporated into user friendly specialist metrics data analysis tools. Eventually tools will become available to allow managers to carry out sophisticated and powerful data analysis routinely. At the moment, though, a simple spreadsheet can add a lot of value for little effort.

A2.9 TIPS AND HINTS

In addition to guidelines, we can offer some hints as to the meaning and interpretation of software product metrics. The following should be taken with some caution but have been found useful and relevant to the environment (real-time telecommunications systems) from which they were taken.

- Provided that comprehensive fault data from all stages of the lifecycle is available in some form, it is possible to model software module correctness with useful accuracy (70–80%), using three types of code metrics (size, information flow, and control flow). Six of these metrics (KLN, HK, NUM, DEP, VIN, and PRA), have been found to be most useful.

- If adequate fault data is not available it may be possible to derive a 'nearly as useful' equivalent measure from a configuration management tool. The measure is : the number of times each module was removed and replaced in the library.

- It is worthwhile to collect accurate effort data during both maintenance and development activities, in particular because surprisingly strong relationships link code characteristics to software maintainability.

- The same factors which appear to cause modules to have more errors in them, also cause them to be less expensive to maintain. Thus while modules with high values of HK are likely to have more faults in them than other modules, the faults which do occur in those modules are also less costly to fix. Linking this with the indication that larger modules tend to be less correct than smaller ones leads to the conclusion that the total maintenance cost of a faulty module may be independent of its size.

- Files requiring change during maintenance tend to have high metric values for both information flow and control flow. Exceptions to this rule are often little-used files.

  This further supports the view that both control flow and information flow measures can be used to highlight troublesome modules. Such static analysis can be performed both before and during maintenance.

- Many structural measures highly correlate with each other which suggests that a subset may be chosen to fully characterise each function at minimal collection cost.

- Outlier analysis is very effective in identifying possible 'hot-spots', such as a function with 32 input parameters.

- The predominant aspect of maintainability (reparability) can be measured in terms of the average fix-effort.

A2.10   WHAT ARE PEOPLE MEASURING?

Finally, we offer a brief overview of what really goes on in software product measurement.

Perhaps the most widely used product metric is that of fault density, which is applied within the context of improving software development processes. Reliability is not commonly measured by developers, and neither is maintainability. Performance is not measured so much as checked against user requirements, as is necessary. The use of product metrics such as size or control flow measures is harder to gauge. Lines of code are of course universally collected, and increasingly non-comment lines of code as well. The routine collection and use of other product metrics is very much tool dependent, and also depends upon the application context. While there have been many older overall quality measurement schemes which incorporate product metrics, they are mainly based upon variations of the McCall quality model [McC77], which has a weak basis in intuition. Their use within current UK quality management schemes is at best advisory.

More recently, in the USA the trend has been to generally apply process metrics to process improvements and to use product metrics in a more controlled and specific way to tackle particular problems. Metrics are not currently used as predictors, except in some cost estimation tools. But what is becoming more common is their incorporation into CASE tools as a part of design improvement. When metrics are buried inside tools in this way there is a tendency for the user of the tool to lose sight of them, although he/she may be benefiting from them indirectly. Another context in which product metrics are being used is as part of testing tools. The interpretation of product metrics remains a problem, however, as there is conflicting evidence concerning their usefulness. Even so, some degree of shared understanding is beginning to emerge [ISO89], albeit far from practical application as yet.

There is now an accumulation of evidence that a method with relatively simple process metrics (e.g. average time taken to fix a fault), if used with rapid feedback loops, can bring about significant quality improvements. The success of such metrics depends mainly upon the mechanisms within which they are introduced. While such benefits are readily available in return for limited setup and reorganisation costs, they are incorrectly perceived as being impractical and overly expensive to realise. In consequence there is still much interest in more sophisticated (if less proven) product metrics in the UK. It would not be unfair to describe this interest as being a desire to run before you can walk, given the proven alternatives available.

Another description might be that it is a search for the silver bullet, the metric which allows dramatic quality improvements to be monitored and planned without organisational disruptions. To date, the only metric even remotely resembling that silver bullet, is still the 'lines of code' metric.

REFERENCES

[BS84] Basili V and Selby R (1984) Data collection and analysis in software research and management *Proc. American Statistical Association, Statistical Computing Section*

[GC92] Grady R and Caswell D (1987) *Software Metrics—Establishing a Company Wide Programme* Prentice-Hall

[Ham85] Hamer PG (1985) *Software Metrics: A Critical Overview* (Volume 13 of Pergamon Infotech State of the Art Report) chapter 16, pp 61–81

[HK81] Henry S and Kafura D (1981) Software structure metrics based on information flow *IEEE Transactions on Software Engineering*, **SE-7** no 5

[IS88] Ince DC and Shepperd M (1988) System design metrics: progress and prospects *Proc IEE/BCS Conference: Software Engineering 88*

[ISO89] ISO Draft Proposal (1989) *Evaluation of Software Product - Software Quality Characteristics and Guideline for their Use.* ISO, DP 9126

[KNP93] Karkaria D, Norris M and Pengelly A (1993) Software assessment *BT Technology Journal* **11** no1

[KP87] Kitchenham BA and Pickard L (1987) Towards a constructive quality model *Software Engineering Journal*

[McC76] McCabe T (1976) A complexity measure *IEEE Transactions on Software Engineering* **SE-2** no4

[McC77] McCall J, Pichards P and Walters G (1977) *Factors in Software Quality* Vols 1, 2 & 3 US Rome air centre reports NTIS AD/A 049 014, 015, 055

Appendix **3**

Process Involvement

Power to the people

John Lennon

This appendix looks at a few of the more useful techniques for drawing on the skills of the people in the project. The methods and approaches outlined here do not supplant good management but they do provide a reasonable framework in which people can contribute to a project's recovery or continued well being.

The first section draws together many of the ideas covered in the main text into a five-stage approach for project improvement. Later sections detail some of the simple but very effective methods that fit within the five-stage approach—Brainstorming, Consensus and Pareto analysis. A more comprehensive list of people-centred approaches is given at the end of the appendix.

A3.1   THE FIVE-STAGE APPROACH

In essence this is a step-by-step process for managing the recovery and improvement of projects. The focus is on the active involvement of the people on the project with the aim of maximising the scope for innovation/creativity of solution—and hence the likelihood of a successful outcome.

In summary, the five stages are:

Stage 1—Recovery/improvement proposal.
Stage 2—Analysis and planning.
Stage 3—Education and communication of action plan.
Stage 4—Detailed implementation plans.
Stage 5—Implementation.

For each of the five stages, there are a number of elements to be addressed and some questions to be answered before moving on to the next stage. In effect, these provide a checklist to be used in conjunction with the main text.

Stage 1—Recovery/improvement proposal

Establishing a clear, specific, well thought out proposal is an essential foundation for success. Your proposal should incorporate:

- *Clear ownership*. This is the key item in any project. An owner, who is totally accountable for the success of some aspect of the project needs to be identified. The owner accepts that any problem in their area is theirs to fix. There needs to be an owner for all problems/tasks identified.

- *Crisp and clear statement of the identified problem*. Including the symptoms of the problem, known defects, failures or errors and any weaknesses in the measurement system.

- *Statement of requirements and objectives*. Describes what needs to be achieved, often either the set of requirements which will be met completely at the end of the project, or a measurable improvement in the progress towards the requirements. Both generally require discussion and agreement with key customers/suppliers.

- *Measurement process*. How the aspects of the problems are to be measured.

- *Targets/milestones*. The ultimate target must be no deviation in meeting the project aims. This may have to be achieved in stages where the target is realistically moved towards the target of 'no deviation'.

Other aspects to consider at this stage are:

- Timing/urgency/links to other initiatives.
- Dependencies (accommodation, materials, etc).
- Impact/visibility.
- Whether you can pull the relevant 'levers'.
- Relationship to achievement of overall operating plan/business plan.

Much of the above is fairly straightforward (indeed obvious). Even so, it is often not done. At this early stage it can be helpful to look at the words you have used in your proposal. Does yours contain words like:

- discover
- devise

- define

- review

- revise?

All of these tend to suggest the need for the sort of initial analysis that should have already been completed as part of the proposal construction process. On the other hand, does it include:

- reduce

- remove/eliminate

- meet target

- improve

- maintain

- do?

All these words suggest that you know what the problem is, how big it is, and that you do intend to do something about it.

Just using the 'right' words to formulate your proposal can have an impact on the ease with which a project gets off the ground and on the chances of managing it to a successful conclusion.

Stage 2—Problem analysis and planning

This is the most important and time consuming part of the process. It requires proper problem analysis whereby the root cause(s) can be identified and solutions can be arrived at based on facts. At the same time it is important that there is a clear understanding of all the people within or outside the organisation who will influence the achievement of the stated requirement. Full use should be made of the structured approaches to problem analysis and solution explained later in this appendix.

The elements of Stage 2 are:

- *Root causes*. The causes of the problem must be defined and the effects of those causes specified using hard data. Theories about the problems and causes must be supported by specific measurements.

- *Possible solutions*. Generate a wide range of possible solutions.

- Selected solution(s). Select one or more of the possible solutions that will best meet the objectives.

- *Problem costs and benefits*. An initial estimate of the project costs and benefits (including predicted reductions in the cost of poor quality).

- *Resource requirements.* Specify any key resource requirements or other dependencies.

- *Planned actions and stages.* Stages 3 and 4 should now be planned out, together with predictions of the results of implementing these plans.

- *Measurements.* Clear measurements must be in place to enable the degree of deviation or failure to be identified and progress tracked.

Now ask yourself the following questions before moving on to Stage 3. Have you:

- Collected all the relevant data?

- Identified the root causes and scheduled the dominant ones for solution?

- Generated a range of possible solutions?

- Selected a solution(s) that best meets the objectives?

- Defined any sub-projects that will arise, and identified their owners?

- Identified the associated costs and benefits (including the existing cost of poor quality) and made a business case for solution?

- Calculated the resource requirements and other major dependencies?

- Developed plans for action including the implications of the chosen solution(s), communication and education of those involved in implementation, and how the gains will be maintained?

- Decided how the project will be measured, including changes to existing measurement systems?

Stage 3—Education and communication of action plan

The achievement of the stated requirements invariably means that a number of people are involved. It is important to identify all those involved or affected (the players and stakeholders) in order that they can fully understand and commit themselves. The check list for this stage is as follows:

- Have you identified all those who could have an effect on the achievement of the requirements?

- What do they need to know and do they need any education or training to help them play their part?

- What is required to ensure cooperation and agreement towards playing their part and are there any guidelines, procedures or practices which would need to be developed to assist them to play their part?

- Do you need to involve them in the appropriate measurements? Can you involve them in developing the appropriate measurements?

Before moving on to the next stage, ask yourself the following questions:

- Whose support/agreement you need to ensure success (e.g. who are the stakeholders in the project)?
- Who needs to be consulted, informed and/or involved (who are 'implements', suppliers, customers)?
- How best to communicate the what, why, when, how, where, by whom?

Have you reviewed:

- Any new evidence about causes or solution(s)?
- How committed the necessary groups are to the solution(s)?
- How able they are to manage the implementation?

Stage 4—Detailed implementation plans

It is at this stage that all those involved have to be brought together within the framework of an overall plan. The planning should cover who does what, by when and with what measurements to ensure that everything is on track for implementation. Everyone should have an opportunity to plan exactly how their part in the implementation should be undertaken.

At completion of Stage 4 is there:

- A detailed implementation plan(s) for all involved stating exactly how they are going to undertake their part of the project?
- Acceptance by the whole team(s) involved?
- Readiness by the team(s) for implementation?

Stage 5—Implementation

This stage is for implementing and measuring and assessing results. It can be a lengthy process because implementation may have to be phased and it inevitably takes time for measurements to confirm that improvements have been achieved.

This stage cannot be considered complete until the measurements confirm a successful solution and/or the benefits are as planned.

Also, the job is not done until recognition has been given to the team—visibly, appropriately, promptly, and personally. Finally, the lessons learned during the improvement/recovery should be recorded for the benefit of subsequent projects.

Summary of the five-stage project approach

Stage 1—Recovery/improvement proposal

Identify:

- Clear ownership
- Crisp and clear statement of problem
- Crisp and clear statement of requirements and objective(s)
- Measurements
- Targets/milestones
- Plan for training and communication.

Stage 2—Problem analysis and planning

Identify:

- Root causes
- Possible solutions
- Selected solution(s)
- Sub projects
- Problem costs and benefits
- Resource requirements
- Planned action and stages
- Measurements.

Stage 3—Education and communication of action plan

- Understanding and involvement of all those affected.
- Identify What, Why, When, Where, How.

Stage 4—Detailed implementation plans

- Action plans
- Commitment and involvement.

Stage 5—Implementation

- Do it
- Measure progress
- Assess results.

A3.2 EXAMPLE TECHNIQUES—BRAINSTORMING

Brainstorming is a technique which encourages creative thinking and the generation of ideas. It is most usefully employed when:

- Generating a list of problems or opportunities
- Identifying possible data requirements
- Developing objectives for solutions
- Generating possible solutions
- Developing action plans.

Providing the rules and principles are carefully followed, brainstorming can produce a great many ideas in a short time and enable participants both to contribute individually and to benefit from the ideas generated by others. Quite often, this seemingly unfocused exercise can encourage the generation of 'unusual' ideas, can establish deeper thinking about particular problems, and unblock long-standing problems. Also it can create the environment which will enhance group activity or teamwork.

Most people have fairly well developed logical thinking skills, which is not surprising since ordinary schooling concentrates on developing this ability. As a result most of us tend to use analytical thinking when confronted with a problem or puzzle and, in many cases, this type of thinking is entirely appropriate. Most software projects do not suffer from a shortage of analytical thinkers!

Many problems, however, require the generation of new ideas, and logical thinking is not especially good at this; some creative or lateral thinking is required. This is especially so in problems where there is no right answer and it is essential to develop a range of alternatives. For instance, how can I sell more products? How can we reduce the number of accidents in the workplace? How can we improve our quality?

Both logical and lateral thinking skills are needed in problem solving and you need to know when it is appropriate to use them. Creative techniques are used to generate alternatives, and logical thinking is used to evaluate them.

There are many barriers to creative thinking, and you need to recognise and overcome them. One of the most important is 'tramline' thinking. We limit our thoughts by what has been done before, or by staying within the boundaries of our present situation. Given this, we tend to make judgements about ideas too soon, and we discard ideas because they seem to be impractical or impossible.

We also tend to make false assumptions about what is, or is not possible or acceptable—'we've always done it like that' or 'they won't accept it' are typical phrases used. We end up assuming that there is only one right answer to a problem.

One barrier that should not be overlooked is the natural fear that people have of seeming foolish. This limits our thoughts to what is seen to be safe and acceptable. It prevents the airing of 'way-out' ideas which are either useful in themselves, or can trigger a good idea from someone else.

The above barriers are overcome by developing the skills of creative or lateral thinking, and brainstorming is perhaps the most widely used technique for this.

There are five basic principles to be followed in brainstorming.

- *No criticism*. This is crucial if barriers to creative thinking are to be overcome. It involves the suspension of evaluation and judgement of ideas and suggestions until after the Brainstorming. It is easier to say than do! The no-criticism rule should apply to the way you think as well as to what you say. Voicing doubts and criticisms will not help the group to overcome the barriers to creativity. Clearing your mind of these things helps you listen and make a more creative input yourself.

- *Freewheel*. This encourages the production of random 'top of the head' ideas. Practicality is not important at this stage; brainstorming is much more effective if outlandish or 'mad' ideas are positively encouraged. It is sometimes worth spending a few minutes concentrating on listing the most way-out ideas concerning the subject being addressed.

- *Quantity*. Generate as many ideas as possible. Brainstorming is about quantity rather than quality in the first instance. It is important to encourage the group to use the ideas generated as a stimulus to their own thinking and to build on others' ideas to produce their own.

- *Record all ideas*. Every idea must be recorded even if it is a repetition expressed in a different way. This should be done in a way that the whole group can see the list as it is being compiled.

- *Incubate*. Take time to reflect on the listed ideas. Often new ideas occur unexpectedly when the mind is occupied elsewhere. Make a note of these and add to the list. Incubation must occur before evaluation.

Once you have decided that brainstorming is an appropriate technique you need to determine who should attend the session. It is important that every participant has a legitimate purpose for attending, and you should include those who need to be there, those who expect to be there and those who can contribute knowledge/experience on the topic.

Remember that people who have nothing to contribute may become frustrated and they may even become disruptive, causing damage to both team building and the generation of ideas. When planning a Brainstorming session you should consider not limiting the attendance to those who have been supportive of past initiatives.

Having assembled the participants explain the purpose and importance of the brainstorming meeting. It is particularly important that you create the right atmosphere for people to express themselves freely.

The purpose should be a concise statement of what is to be achieved by the brainstorming, and the best way of getting a team to address the objectives is in the form of a question such as 'What are all the ways of...?' or 'How could we...?'

The agreed purpose of the meeting should be posted on the wall of the room, and should help to answer certain questions from those taking part, notably:

- 'Why is this session important to me as leader of the group?'

- 'Why is this session important to you as participants?'

- 'Why is this session important to the business unit?'

At the start of the session, the briefing should ensure that all the participants understand:

- The roles within the group: who is the leader; who will record the ideas as they are produced?

- The time allocated to each step.

- That it may not be possible/desirable to complete the process in one meeting. In this case the participants will need to agree how they are to progress towards the incubation and subsequent evaluation of ideas.

Once under way, the first phase of the brainstorming session is to start the ideas coming. There are several ways of doing this. In turn each member of the group can offer an idea (or pass); ideas can be written on cards and passed to a recorder; or a combination of these can be used; or a group can devise its own methods. Make sure that all ideas are recorded and that the full list is visible to all of the group. And leave some time for the dust to settle (incubate the ideas that have been generated).

If more than one meeting is necessary it may help the process to post the lists/diagrams in the work area to ensure both participants and interested non-participants can see the results and add to the information if they wish. It also keeps the issues live which helps with the incubation.

The last step is to evaluate the ideas. Having generated a number of ideas the next step is to evaluate their usefulness towards meeting the original objective. Trying to deal with a random list of ideas may be difficult, and some initial classification may be necessary.

One approach is to collect ideas into sets having a common theme, and each set can then be evaluated using the Plus, Minus and Interesting routine. To use this approach the group allocates a Plus to sets with the most promising ideas, a Minus to the least promising, and an Interesting rating to those in between.

This routine can also be applied to individual ideas in a set. Whichever approach you take, do not discard any of the ideas as they may prove to be useful later.

After the session, it is vital to handle summary and follow-up action. It is important that the brainstorming session is seen in context, and that participants recognise the importance of their input and their continuing involvement with the process. An explanation of the group's future role should be given, and be reinforced by identifying follow-up dates and mapping out the future progress of the project.

Brainstorming generates the possibilities. The next technique looks at how decisions on those options can be made.

A3.3   EXAMPLE TECHNIQUES—CONSENSUS

Consensus Reaching is a technique which (through a structured approach) helps a group of people to arrive at an agreed decision. It enables every member in a group to actively contribute to a decision.

During the process each member is given the opportunity to make known their views to the group. By the time consensus has been reached, every member of the group will have a clear understanding of all other's points of view. As a result, the selected viewpoint will achieve a high degree of acceptance and commitment by each member.

You should not assume total commitment from a group of people who have not been involved in making a decision. If you make a decision without consulting those whom it will affect then you cannot expect their support in carrying that decision through. Decision making is a major part of any project and possibly the most difficult activity undertaken. Accepting an input from those who have relevant knowledge to contribute will help you go forward with the best decision.

There are different methods of involving people in decision making; these are:

- *Majority decision* . Take a vote and count those in favour. What you end up with is the view of the majority. But there is a high probability that those people who voted against the decision will not be committed to the majority's viewpoint.

- *Decision by minority* . Select a number of people to make a decision on behalf of the group. The decision made by these people can be difficult to operate, because it is most likely that their views will not be representative of the whole group. The ultimate in minority decision making—autocracy—rarely achieves the best result.

- *Unanimous decision* . Everybody agrees with the decision and you have total commitment. Everyone in the group is of one mind and there is no need to compromise any of the viewpoints. It is the ideal solution that in reality is rarely achieved.

- *Consensus decision* . This is a very practical method of decision making, and sits between unanimous and majority decision methods. Having first discussed all the alternatives, a vote can be taken, which will indicate favour for either one or more decisions. The group will then be given the opportunity to discuss the options. The process of voting and discussion will need to continue until consensus has been reached on one decision.

By nature, some people are reluctant to contribute in an open discussion and often the strong-willed person will impose their point of view. As a result, some people within the group will tend to tolerate the decision rather than support it. This would mean that implementation of the decision could meet with unnecessary difficulties

Consensus reaching allows each person within a group to contribute to the decision making process. Reaching a decision by consensus means that each person present supports the decision. Remember, a majority agreement is not consensus, everybody has to agree!

To summarise, consensus reaching has a five-step approach, where the first four steps are preparatory to the fifth step in which consensus is reached. The steps are:

- List ideas/suggestions.

- Record ideas/suggestions.

- Check understanding.

- Vote on ideas/suggestions.

- Reach a consensus.

To perform consensus reaching you should prepare the session by getting the group together, explaining the technique and check understanding with each person, asking somebody (preferably outside the group) to act as a 'scribe' and providing paper, pencils, flip chart and voting/star stickers. Then the following steps should be followed:

Step 1—List ideas/suggestions

The purpose of this step is to collect ideas (e.g. solutions to problem) from each person in the group. It can be done by using either of the following methods:

- Get each person to write down their ideas on a sheet of paper. You may wish to provide pre-printed forms.

- Use brainstorming to collect ideas from the group. You may need to review the rules of brainstorming. The method that you choose should be based on your knowledge of the individuals within the group and the task the group is addressing.

Step 2—Record ideas/suggestions

Having gathered all of the ideas, display them to the group. If the group listed their ideas, invite each person in turn to read them out. The scribe will write them down on a flip chart. Do not encourage any judgement or evaluation at this stage.

If Brainstorming was used to gather the ideas, then they will have been recorded on a flip chart by the scribe during that session.

Whichever method used, encourage the group to add new ideas as they think of them.

Step 3—Check understanding

Now that the ideas are recorded, you should ensure that everybody in the group understands all the ideas on the flip chart.

Discuss each idea with the group, asking the person whose idea is being discussed to clarify on points raised by the group. Remember, this discussion is to check understanding and not to evaluate or judge.

Step 4—Vote on ideas/suggestions

Label each idea with a number or letter. Ask each person to assign the ideas with a score and to record these scores on a piece of paper. There are two usual methods of scoring:

- If there are, say 20 ideas, then start with 20 points for the idea valued most, down to one point allocated to the idea least thought of.

- Again assuming twenty ideas, each person can award a total of twenty points as they see fit. They could award all twenty points to one idea, or spread them over a number of ideas. There is no need to vote on every idea. This method of scoring is known as 'weighted'.

Full use should be made of voting stickers, stars and 'post-its' in order that the group can openly indicate to each other their preference.

Step 5—Reach a consensus

This step achieves the objective of the technique by getting everybody to agree and support one of the ideas.

Invite each person in turn to read out their scores. The scribe will record the scores against each chosen idea on the flip chart. Total the points for each idea and mark those which have gained the highest score. This will indicate the majority view of the group, and is a good starting point for discussion.

Ask each person in turn, to tell the group the reason why they gave a particular idea their highest score. After everybody has done this, ask the group if anyone wishes to change their scores. The scribe will record these changes. And so the process continues, with more discussion and re-scoring.

Consensus reaching is a very powerful technique, so be patient, and use it properly! You may well find out that an idea which initially received a small number of votes, becomes the one on which consensus is reached.

Throughout the process your purpose has been to get the group to agree a decision. It may not be the one a particular individual had favoured, but each person now accepts why the group should support that decision.

It is important that the team leader checks that all team members visibly support the implementation of the agreed/chosen decision.

A3.4 EXAMPLE TECHNIQUES—PARETO ANALYSIS

So far we have, in essence, a technique for generating ideas and one for getting people's buy-in to them. The final technique explained in this appendix —Pareto Analysis—is suited to the evaluation of proposed solutions.

Pareto is an adept at separating the 'vital few' from the 'useful many'.

'First things first' is the thought behind Pareto; the properly constructed diagram generated through Pareto analysis should suggest the error or activity on which resources should be used first to make the best improvement.

Very often the simple process of arranging data may suggest something of importance that would otherwise have gone unnoticed. Selecting classifications, tabulating data, ordering data, and constructing a Pareto diagram have often served a useful purpose in problem investigation.

The communication process between people takes on many forms, and Pareto diagrams are a form of language using a display in a commonly understood format. The continued use of the Pareto diagram can also enhance communication between project members.

Pareto diagrams can be used to illustrate progress. Comparing Pareto diagrams drawn at key milestones during the solution of a problem would enable the effectiveness of the corrective action to be evaluated. Changing conditions may cause a reordering of the data classes, or changes in the shape of the cumulative line. These changes can be highlighted by using colours or transparent overlays, or by presenting the diagrams in sequence.

Cumulative lines are convenient for answering questions such as, 'What types of fault or error constitute 50% of all defects?'. Pareto diagrams are useful in organizing data in preparation for the construction of the cumulative line.

Analysis often reveals that, for example, a small number of failures are responsible for the bulk of quality costs. This conforms to the so-called 'Pareto Principle', named after the Italian economist who discovered that the majority of his country's wealth was owned by relatively few people.

In many situations a similar pattern becomes apparent when we look at the relationship between numbers of items and their contribution to the extent of the problem. This pattern has been referred to as the 80/20 rule and shows itself in many ways. 80% of your telephone calls, for instance, come from 20% of your colleagues; similarly 80% of a company's failure costs probably result from 20% of its problem areas.

The 80/20 principle does not mean that exactly 80% of the total problem is provided for by 20% of the features but that there is usually a similarly large imbalance. The ratio itself is not as important as the fact that it is the major causes that are being identified.

In other words, amongst the wide range of problems that you may be faced with, there are a few vital ones which must be tackled immediately, and many others which can be dealt with later. Pareto analysis shows at a glance which problem areas can be regarded as a 'vital few', needing special measures to tackle them, and which are the 'useful many'.

In most cases the identification of the 'vital few' does not come as a complete surprise. On the contrary, some of the problems on the list will have long been notorious, but the big accomplishments of the Pareto analysis are that:

- Some notorious problems are confirmed as belonging to the 'vital few'.

- Some problems, previously not notorious, are identified as belonging to the 'vital few'.

- The 'useful many' are identified: this is not new but the extent is usually shocking—the real size of the problem is revealed.

- A basis for sorting the problems is established.

There are five steps to Pareto Analysis:

- List the activities to be analysed.

- Calculate totals.

- Order totals.

- Draw the Pareto diagrams.

- Interpret results.

These steps can be explained with reference to Table A3.1:

- *List the errors/activities to be analysed*. Begin by making a list of the errors or activities to be analysed (Column 1 in the table) and for each of them count the number of times each occurs (Column 2 in table).

- *Calculate totals*. Calculate the total for the whole list, and the percentage that each item represents of this total (Column 3 in table).

● *Order totals*. List the errors/activities starting with the largest, and calculate the cumulative percentage as you go down the list (Column 4 in the Table). You will end with the smallest item which will make up the final element of the 100%.

Table A3.1   Typical analysis of errors

Error	Frequency	% of Total	Cumulative
A	110	40.2	40.2
B	63	23.1	63.3
C	47	17.2	80.5
D	28	10.3	90.8
E	19	7.0	97.8
F	6	2.2	100

● *Draw the Pareto diagrams*. Draw a bar chart as shown in the Figure A3.2. The vertical scale shows the volume of what it is you are comparing and the horizontal scale breaks this down into meaningful categories, so you can tell which category is causing the greatest problem. For example, error A was counted 110 times, and this is represented by bar A on the chart.

    When many types of defects are involved the horizontal scale of your Pareto diagram may become very wide. Put minor errors together and call them 'others', and this will narrow your horizontal scale.

    In choosing the data to be charted keep in mind the purpose that your diagram will serve. The proper selection of data for the vertical scale and for categories on the horizontal scale is of vital importance. The right

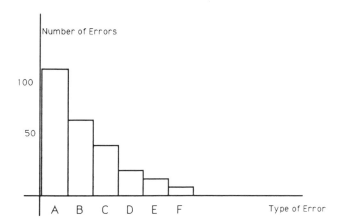

Figure A3.2   A Pareto diagram

selections bring attention to the most troublesome problems. The wrong selections can be misleading and result in wasted time.

In this case, for example, it appears that error A deserves the priority attention. However, if we consider the cost of each error, the rankings may change. To illustrate this point assume that each of the six errors listed has associated costs as in Table A3.3: Now calculate the total cost for each error as shown below and you will see that the ranking of the errors has changed significantly, as in Tables A3.4 and A3.5. Redrawing the Pareto diagram, using the costs figures for the vertical scale, instead of the frequency figures, we obtain the revised Pareto diagram as in Figure A3.6.

Table A3.3   Costs of each error

Error	Cost/item
A	0.45
B	1.11
C	6.38
D	1.07
E	7.98
F	2.00

Table A3.4   Combined cost of errors

Error	Cost/item	Number	Total cost	Previous	New
A	0.45	110	49.5	1	4
B	1.11	63	69.93	2	3
C	6.38	47	299.86	3	1
D	1.07	28	29.96	4	5
E	7.98	19	149.91	5	2
F	2.00	6	12.0	6	6

Table A3.5   Revised analysis of errors

Error	Total cost	% of Total	Cumulative
C	300	49.0	49.0
E	150	24.5	73.5
B	70	11.4	84.9
A	50	8.2	93.1
D	30	4.9	98.0
F	12	2.0	100

The Pareto diagram can be enhanced by drawing in the cumulative curve as shown in the diagram below. The first step is to draw in the cumulative bars; the first bar is simply the largest item by itself—in this case error C. The next cumulative bar represents error C added to error E bars C and E combined, and so on until all the bars have been included. The next step is to draw the cumulative curve and this is done by joining the top right hand corner of each bar. Finally provide a second scale at the right hand margin of the Pareto diagram with zero on the vertical axis, and 100% aligned with the top of the overall cumulative bar as in Figure A3.7.

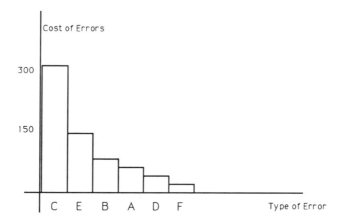

Figure A3.6   Revised Pareto diagram

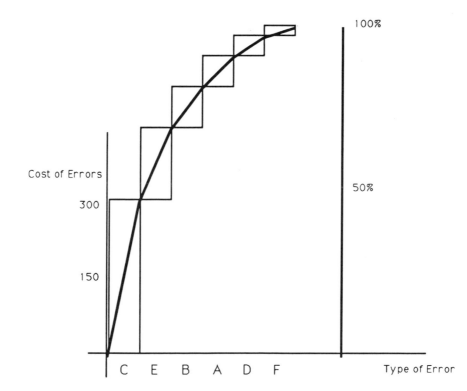

Figure A3.7   The cumulative curve

- *Interpret Results.* The candidates for priority action, the 'vital few' will appear on the left of the Pareto diagram where the slope of the cumulative curve will be steepest.

    The 'useful many' should not be ignored. Sometimes an apparent triviality now can become significant later. It is important to examine the 'useful many' for any such 'time bombs'. In this first pass, though, these can wait.

    There may be some problems about which it is difficult to collect specific numeric data such as issues concerning morale, or customer image. In these cases it may be necessary to rely more heavily on subjective decisions about which problems are the 'vital few' to be marked out for special treatment. This type of subjective Pareto analysis can be extremely powerful in its own right, especially when twinned with the use of cause and effect diagrams.

As stated earlier on, the Pareto principle is not normally used in isolation. It is best applied in conjunction with brainstorming and consensus as part of the overall problem solving process. The three together provide a simple but effective framework for bringing people together and focusing their minds on the building of a healthy project.

A3.5   OTHER TECHNIQUES

The techniques detailed above are but three of many. We now mention a wider selection which can be used during project recovery and improvement. All of those covered have their merits and the literature referenced at the end of the appendix contains pointers to the most appropriate technique for a given situation

An *Action Plan* is an outline of who will do what, when and how to achieve a specific objective. It forms a basis to 'get it right first time'.

Activity sampling is a work measurement technique which provides reasonably accurate data on the proportion of time being devoted to each type of activity within a job. It relies on the results obtained from a sample consisting of a number of individual moments selected at random intervals from a representative period of the job.

Cause and effect analysis is a technique for identifying the possible causes affecting a project/problem. A *cause and effect diagram* is a visually effective way of recording causes as they are suggested.

A *Checklist* is a list of things to be done or items to be obtained. It is a simple way of remembering what to do and then checking that you have done it.

Completed staffwork is the total analysis and preparation of a task, opportunity or problem by a review/team so that after their presentation of the solution all that remains to be done by the next level of management is to agree the action/solution proposed.

Concentration diagrams are used to show the location of events or problems. They are sometimes called defect location diagrams or defect location check-sheets.

A *Contingency Plan* is an outline of the what, who, when, and how which needs to be addressed to ensure that any potential barriers to the implementation of a project are handled in a pro-active manner.

Control Comparison is a technique for comparing the problem situation with an identical or similar situation, the 'control', where the problem does not exist, to assist in identifying the root cause.

Cost benefit analysis is a technique for comparing the costs of taking a particular course of action with the benefits achievable from the outcome. It is a method of assessing the viability of the course of action in monetary terms.

Cost of poor quality is a technique that has been developed to identify the need and opportunities for quality improvement in a language we all understand—money. A cost of poor quality exercise identifies where opportunities exist for improvement and the cost penalties to the business when we fail to get it right first time.

Critical Path Method is a technique for analysing the work to be done on a project into identifiable tasks at an early stage. The sequence in which the tasks are to be performed is shown by a network of arrows, with each arrow representing a particular task. A time estimate is added for each task and, by simple arithmetic, dates can be calculated for each stage of the project. The network and the information it contains can then be used to plan and control a project. The sequence of tasks, which forms the longest time path through the network and therefore dictates the overall time required to complete the project, is known as the Critical Path.

Customer perceptions—the process of finding out what our external and internal customers think of our products and services, usually expressed as a simple rating across key categories (e.g. accuracy of reporting, value for money, etc).

Decision Analysis is a technique to assist you, or a group, to determine the choice of an action to take, taking account of, for example, the objectives, what alternatives there are and what risks are involved.

Department purpose analysis (DPA) is designed to ensure that a department or group is achieving goals that contribute to the company's strategy and overall goals, and that the department's activities actually add value. A key step in the process is a clear focus on agreeing, measuring and meeting customer requirements—in lay terms DPA seeks to discriminate useful activity from irrelevant flapping.

Effective meetings—the process of conducting meetings successfully to ensure effective teamwork, quality decision making, enhanced communication, improved morale and optimum efficiency.

Employee perceptions—is the process of finding out what our managers and staff think of the company and how it operates. It usually covers how effective management is perceived to be, how viable policy/strategy is considered, how motivated people feel, etc.

Flowcharts—the representation of processes, systems or procedures by means of diagrams with symbols indicating, for example, actions and decisions.

Force field analysis is a technique for identifying the forces that help or obstruct a change you want to make.

Gaining support is a technique which provides you with a set of guidelines when enlisting the support of others who are affected by your project or process.

A *milestone plan* is an outline of the when and what in the staged implementation of, say, an action plan.

Potential problem analysis is a technique which will help you anticipate problems before they happen and to identify the actions needed to be taken, to prevent them from happening, or to minimise their effect.

Problem analysis is a technique which will enable you to think logically and find root causes of difference—positive or negative—in standards of performance within a management or work process.

A *Problem definition sheet* is a means of providing a clear statement of a problem, its aims and the objectives that are required to overcome the problem. It includes an assessment of costs and benefits, and likely timescales for solving and implementation.

Process analysis is a technique which will enable you to produce a fully detailed picture of a process with all the steps clearly identified. You will be able to go on to review each step in the process, identify problems and opportunities, and to pursue these through a systematic approach. The review will also highlight opportunities for you to increase the effective control of the process.

Project Selection is a systematic approach to ensure that a project is selected that is worthwhile. It includes the use of project selection criteria of: importance, measurement, feasibility, cost effectiveness and time.

The *rating sheet* provides a method of deciding on one option when a number of alternatives exist.

Sampling is a means by which a small group of items (the sample), are taken from a larger group (the population) so as to be representative of the larger group.

REFERENCES

The following are given as general rather than specific references as they cover many of the areas covered in this appendix.

Adair J (1986) *Action Centred Leadership* Gower Publishing
Buzan T (1986) *Use Your Head* BBC Publications
de Bono E (1986) *Lateral Thinking* Penguin
de Bono E (1986) *Six Thinking Hats* Penquin
Fordyce JK and Weil R (1986) *Managing with People* Addison-Wesley
Galbraith JK (1983) *Getting to Yes* Hutchinson & Co
Juran JM (1984) *Managerial Breakthrough* McGraw-Hill
Kanter RM (1987) *The Change Masters* Unwin Paperbacks

Glossary

The definitions given here are intended to help clarify some of more common terms and concepts used in the context of software projects. These are not formal definitions, rather a brief explanation of what each term is about.

Abstraction   A representation of something that contains less information than the something. For example, a data abstraction provides information about some referent in the outside world without indicating how the data are represented in the computer.

Abstract   Containing less information than reality.

Ada   A programming language, developed under the leadership of the U.S. Department of Defence, specifically oriented to support modern software development practices.

Algorithm   A precise set of instructions for carrying out some computation (e.g., the algorithm for calculating an employee's take-home pay).

Application   The user task performed by a computer (such as making a hotel reservation, processing a company's accounts or analysing market research data).

Applications software   The software used to carry out the applications task.

Architect   The person responsible for creating the structure in a system (e.g. its organisation into major parts). A Chief Architect would be responsible for the overall design of a major system.

Artificial intelligence (AI)   Applications that would appear to show intelligence if they were carried out by a human being.

Assembler   A program, usually provided by the computer manufacturer, to translate a program written in assembly language to machine code. In general, each assembly language instruction is changed into one machine-code instruction. (Also called an Assembly Program)

Assembly   The process of converting a program written in assembly language into machine code.

Assembly language   A low-level programming language, generally using symbolic addresses, which is translated into machine code by an assembler.

Assessor   A person who is qualified and is authorised to perform all or any portion of a quality system assessment. The term Auditor can also be used.

Automation   Systems that can operate with little or no human intervention. It is easiest to automate simple mechanical processes, hardest to automate those tasks needing common sense, creative ability, judgement or initiative in unprecedented situations.

Bug   An error in program or fault in equipment.

Cobol   A programming language oriented toward business data processing.

Code   A computer program expressed in the machine language of the computer on which it will be executed, i.e. the executable form of a program. More generally, a program expressed in a representation that requires only trivial changes to make it ready for execution.

Compiler   A program which translates a high-level language program into a computer's machine code or some other low-level language. Each high-level language instruction is changed into several machine-code instructions. It produces an independent program which is capable of being executed by itself. This process is known as compilation.

Components   Parts of a program or computer system.

Computer   A piece of hardware that can store and execute instructions (i.e. interpret them and cause some action to occur).

Configuration   A collection of items that bear a particular relation to each other (e.g. the data configuration of a system in which classes of data and their relationships are defined).

Cross assembler A program, written for one computer, which assembles a program written for a second computer, usually a smaller one such as a microcomputer, and outputs machine-code instructions suitable to be executed on the second computer.

Cross compiler A program, written for one computer, which compiles a program written for a second computer usually a smaller one such as a microcomputer, and outputs appropriate machine-code instructions suitable to be executed on the second computer.

Customer A person or entity paying for a piece of software. There are many different types of customer and these are detailed in the main text

Data Usually the same as information. Sometimes information is regarded as processed data.

Data design The design of the data structure needed by a particular software system.

Data preparation The conversion of data (perhaps collected manually) to make it suitable for subsequent computer input.

Debugging The detection, location and correction of bugs.

Diagnostic aid An aid in the debugging of programs, e.g. a trace program.

Diagnostic program One that attempts to detect and locate faults in a computer system.

Design (n) A plan for a program or piece of software.

Design (v) To create a design; to plan and structure a technical artefact.

Development A set of activities that are carried out to create a piece of software (e.g. design, programming, and testing).

DoD The U.S. Department of Defense.

Editor A program which enables users to inspect and alter their program or data.

Engineering A process of applying scientific and other information in specific ways to achieve technical, economic, and human goals.

Error A fault or mistake causing the failure of a computer program or causing a system to produce expected results.

Error Message   An indication that an error has been detected.

Evolution   Changes to a piece of software after its initial development; typically, this is repair of problems, adaptation to new conditions, and enhancement with new functionality. Sometimes called maintenance.

Feedback   Information from some process that is sent back to the entity carrying out the process in order that some variables of the process can be changed. *'Feedback from the customers gave the development group several ideas on how to improve the system they were producing.'*

Function   A special duty or performance of a thing or a person (e.g. the function of the programmer is to create programs; the function of a compiler is to translate programs from one language to another).

Functional specification   The definition of a piece of software in terms of the functions it is intended to perform.

Hardware   The physical equipment in a computer system. It is usually contrasted with software.

Heuristic program   One which attempts to improve its own performance as a result of learning from previous actions within a program.

High-level programming language   A problem-oriented language, in which instructions may be equivalent to several machine-code instructions, and which may be used on different computers by using an appropriate compiler. Common examples are Pascal, Cobol, Fortran and C.

Implementation   The process of converting the notation used to express detailed software design into the program code (also known as coding or programming). Implementation also denotes the task of bringing together the various systems components to get the system working (also known as commissioning).

Interface   The boundary between two things, typically two programs, two pieces of hardware, a computer and its user, a project manager and the customer.

Interpreter   A program which translates and executes a source program one statement at a time.

Key   The record identifier used in many information retrieval systems.

Language   An agreed-upon set of symbols, rules for combining them, and meanings attached to the symbols that is used to express something (e.g. the

Pascal programming language, job- control language for an operating system, and a graphical language for building models of a proposed piece of software).

Lead assessor   An Assessor who is qualified and is authorised to manage a quality system assessment.

Lifecycle   A defined set of stages through which a piece of software passes over time—from requirements analysis to maintenance.

Low-level programming language   A machine-oriented language in which each program instruction is close to a single machine-code instruction.

Machine-code instruction   One which directly defines a particular machine operation and can be recognised and executed without any intermediate translation.

Maintenance   Changes to a piece of software after its initial development; also called evolution. In practice, it is the task of modifying (locating problems, correcting or updating, etc) a software system after it has been put into operation.

Method   A way of doing something. In software terms it is generally a defined approach to achieving the various phases of the lifecycle. Methods are usually regarded as functionally similar to tools (e.g. a specific tool will support a particular method).

Model   An abstraction of reality that still bears enough resemblance to the object of the model that we can answer some questions about the object by consulting the model.

Modelling   Simulation of a system by manipulating a number of interactive variables; can answer 'what if...?' questions to predict the behaviour of the modelled system. A model of a system or subsystem is often called a prototype.

Modularisation   The splitting up of a software system into a number of manageable sections (modules) to ease design, coding, etc.

Object program   The translated versions of a program that has been assembled or compiled.

Objectives   Targets for action, such that we can tell when they have been met (e.g. the objective of producing software that incurs no more than three fatal errors in the first year of operation).

Operating system   The software that controls a computer system. It allows a number of programs to be run on the computer at the same time without the need for operator intervention.

Operation code   The part of a machine-code instruction that specifies the operation to be performed.

Parameter   A variable whose value may change the operation but not the structure of some activity (e.g. an important parameter in the productivity of a program is the language used).

Phases   Individual stages of work on a piece of software (e.g. the testing phase).

Procedure   A method or set of steps defining an activity; technically a program that can be executed as a subactivity by another program.

Process   Technically, a procedure that is being executed on a specific set of data; more generally, a procedure for doing something that is actually being carried out.

Processor   That part of a computer capable of executing instructions. More generally, any active agent capable of carrying out a set of instructions (e.g. a transaction processor for modifying a database).

Product   Usually, an entity to be sold; more generally, the end result of some process.

Program   A set of instructions for a computer, arranged so that when executed they will cause some desired effect (such as the calculation of a quantity or the retrieval of a piece of data).

Programming language   An artificial language constructed in such a way that people and programmable machines can communicate with each other in a precise and intelligible way.

Project management   The systematic approach for analysing, organising and completing a project, of whatever type.

Prototype   A scaled-down version of something, built before the complete item is built, in order to assess the feasibility or utility of the full version.

Quality assessment   A systematic and independent examination to determine whether quality activities and related results comply with planned arrangements and whether these arrangements are implemented effectively and are suitable to achieve objectives.

Quality surveillance   The continuing monitoring and verification of the status of procedures, methods, conditions, processes, products and services, and the analysis of records in relation to stated references to ensure that specified requirements for quality are being met.

Quality system   The organisational structure, responsibilities, procedures, processes and resources for implementing quality management.

Quality system standards   A quality system standard is a document specifying the elements of a quality system.

Requirements analysis   The analysis of a user's needs and the conversion of these into a statement of requirements, prior to specification.

Run-time system   The complete set of software which must be in primary storage while a user program is being executed.

Second party assessments   Assessments of contractors/ suppliers undertaken on behalf of a purchasing organisation. This may include the assessment of companies or divisions supplying goods or services to others within the same group.

Segmentation   The process of dividing a program into sections (segments or modules), which may be independently executed or independently changed.

Software   Programs, data, designs for programs, specifications, and any of the other information that is relevant to a particular set of executable computer instructions (either existing or planned).

Software engineering   The development and use of systematic strategies (themselves often software based) for the production of good quality software within budgets and to timescales.

Software package   A fully documented program, or set of programs, designed to perform a particular task.

Source program   The program as written by the programmer using a programming language; it must be assembled, compiled or interpreted into object code before it can be executed.

Specification   A description of a system or program that states what should be provided but does not necessarily provide information on exactly how the system or program will work.

Standard function   A sub-program provided by a computer or other translator which carries out a task such as the computation of a mathematical function (e.g. log, sine, square root).

Structure   *'The structure of the program was very poor,"* means that the outline of the program, as represented by the major paths of its possible flow of control, was poor, which in turn usually means that it was jumbled, had many alternatives, that the connection between different regions of the program was unclear, and so on.

Structured programming   An orderly approach to programming which emphasises breaking large and complex tasks into successively smaller section.

Subsystem   A system contained within a larger system; usually the subsystem can 'stand alone' (e.g. the programming subsystem in a development organisation).

Syntax   The set of rules for combining the elements of a language (e.g. words) into permitted constructions (e.g. phrases and sentences). The set of rules does not define meaning, nor does it depend on the use made of the final construction.

System   A collection of elements that work together, forming a coherent whole (e.g. a computer system consisting of processors, printers, disks, etc.).

System design   The process of establishing the overall architecture of a software system.

Systems program   One of the programs which control the performance of a computer system (e.g. Compiler or Monitor).

Systems software   Software, such as an operating system, concerned mainly with 'house-keeping' tasks, managing the hardware resources, etc. It is usually contrasted with applications software.

Test data   Data used to test a program or flow-chart; as well as the data, the expected results are specified.

Testing   The process of executing software with test data to check that it satisfies the specification. Testing is a major part of validation.

Third party assessments   Assessments of organisations undertaken by an independent certification body or similar organisation.

Tool   Any artefact that can be used to amplify the power of a human being in developing software; usually refers to a tangible object such as a terminal or a program (e.g. a test-case generator).

Trace   A means of checking the logic of a program by inserting statements which cause the values of variables or other information to be printed out as the program is executed.

Transformation   A change of one aspect or form of software into another form (e.g. the transformation of specifications for a program into the design of a program that fulfills the specifications).

Utility program   A systems program designed to perform a common task such as transferring data from one storage device to another or for editing text.

Validation   The process of checking a specific piece of lifecycle notation, and the conversion from one piece of notation to another (see also Testing).

Verification   The process of proving that a program meets its specification.

Waterfall   The name for the 'classical' software lifecycle, so named because the chart used to portray it suggests a waterfall.

Bibliography

Most of the chapters within this book have brief lists of relevant references at the end. This bibliography aims to supplement these lists with useful texts (some repeated for emphasis!).

Abbott R J (1986) *An Integrated Approach to Software Development* John Wiley & Sons

Abbott R J (1986), *Software Development* John Wiley & Sons

AMI Handbook (1992) *Applications of Metrics in Industry* Esprit COSMOS Project

Babich, W A (1985) *Software Configuration Management: Coordination and Control for Productivity*, Addison-Wesley

BCS Trends in IT Series (1989) *The Future Impact of Information Technology* British Computer Society

Boehm B W (1981) *Software Engineering Economics* Prentice-Hall

Brooks F P (1975) *The Mythical Man-Month: Essays on Software Engineering* Addison-Wesley

Burton and Shelton (1992) *Software Solutions* Houghton Mifflin

Crosby P B (1980) *Quality is Free: The Art of Making Quality Certain* Mentor (New American Library)

Fairley R (1985) *Software Engineering Concepts* McGraw-Hill

Gall J (1975) *Systemantics: How Systems Work and Especially How They Fail* Pocket Books

Glass R L and Noiseux R A (1981) *Software Maintenance Guidebook* Prentice-Hall

Grady R and Caswell D (1987) *Software Metrics - Establishing a Company wide Programme* Prentice-Hall

Gunther R C (1978) *Management Methodology for Software Product Engineering* Wiley-Interscience

Jones C (1986) *Programming Productivity* McGraw-Hill

Lehman M M and Belady L A (1985) *Program Evolution: Processes of Software Change* Academic Press

Lientz B P and Swanson E B (1980) *Software Maintenance Management* Addison-Wesley

Luce D and Andrews D (1990) *The Software Lifecycle* Butterworth Heinemann

Marciniak J J and Reifer D J (1990) *Software Acquisition Management* John Wiley & Sons

McDermid J (1991) *Software Engineers Reference Book*, Butterworth Heinemann

Musa J D, Iannino A and Okumoto K (1987) *Software Reliability: Measurement, Prediction, Application* McGraw-Hill

Nasbitt J (1982) *Megatrends: Ten New Directions Transforming Our Lives* Warner Books

Peters L (1981) *Software Design: Methods and Techniques* Yourdon Press

Peters T J and Waterman R H Jr *In search of Excellence* Harper and Row

Pressman R (1987) *Software Engineering: A Practitioner's Approach, 2nd Edition* McGraw-Hill

Sharp A (1993) *Software Quality and Productivity* Von Nostrand Reinhold

STARTS Public Purchaser Group (1986) with the support of the DTI and NCC *The STARTS Purchasers' Handbook*

Veryard R (1991) *The Economics of Information and Systems Software* Butterworth Heinemann

Weinberg G (1971) *Psychology of Computer Programming* Van Nostrand Reinhold

Yourdon E (1993) *Decline and Fall of the American Programmer* Prentice-Hall

Index